EDUCATION AND CHALLENGES OF GLOBALISATION

EDUCATION AND CHALLENGES OF GLOBALISATION

Editor
Prof. Ramesh Chandra

Publications
KALPAZ PUBLICATIONS
DELHI-110052

Education and Challenges of Globalisation

ISBN: 81-7835-229-X

This book is Vol. No. 1 of Universal Education and Technology in 21st Century (Set)

Published in 2007 in India by
Kalpaz Publications,
C-30, Satyawati Nagar, Delhi-110052
E-mail : Kalpaz@hotmail.com
Ph : 9212729499

Laser Typesetting at : Master Computers, Delhi
Printed at : Rajdhani Printers, Delhi

Contents

Preface

1. **Education: Evolutionary Concept** 1
A Framework for Thinking: Regulating the Global Space of Higher Education; International Cooperation in Higher Education and Training; Globalisation, Internationalisation and Europeanisation; Key Themes and Trends in the Current Debate on International Cooperation in Higher Education; Academic Staff-Mobility; Internationalising Curricula; Recognition and Transparency; Institutional and Strategic Integration of International Cooperation Activities; Institutional Networking; Internationalisation and Quality Assurance; The Impact of Neo Technologies on Internationalisation; Trends.

2. **Challenges of Globalisation Education** 74
Tertiary Education Policy in the Context of the World Bank's Development Strategy; Poverty Reduction through Redistribution and Empowerment; Fulfillment of Millennium Development Goals; The State and Territory Education; Externalities; Equity; Support for other Levels of the Education System; Determining Appropriate Investment Levels; The Evolving Role of the State; World Bank Support for Tertiary Education; Directions for Future Bank Support; Facilitating Policy

Dialogue and Knowledge Sharing; Enabling Framework for Global Public Goods; Globalisation Apartheid—The Role of Higher Education in Development; Higher Education and Development; Promoting Cooperation within a Competitive Environment.

3. **Implications of Quality Education** 115
Why Globalisation?; Travel; Free Trade Zones; Multinational Companies; Education; Mobility of Education; The Business of Education; Education at a Distance; Transnational Education; On-line Education: The 'Virtual University'; Distance Education On-line; Collaborative Education; Supping with the Devil: Academia/business Collaboration; Mobility and Recognition; Recognition of Qualifications; Employability; The Role of Professional Associations; Contradictions; Trade and Education; Implications for Quality; A Global Accreditor; Mutual Recognition of the Activities of QA Agencies; A Quality Hallmark; the Flexible QA Agency; Universities in the New Global Economy; Internationalisation or Globalisation of Higher Education?; Internationalisation; Globalisation and Higher Education.

4. **Universities in Globalisation** 148
Training and Research Programmes; Adaptation of Our Institutions; Universities in the Era of Globalisation; Globalisation and National University Systems.

5. **Globalisation and Higher Education Challenges** 174
Changes and Challenges in the Provision of Higher Education; Purpose of GATS; Major

Principles; Extent of Country Commitments; Trade Liberalisation and Trends in Higher Education; Mobility of Professionals; Culture and Acculturation; Trade Dominates; New Models for Higher Education; A Teaching/ Learning Model; Active Learning; A Learning Environment Based on Collaboration; A Unique Program Format; On-campus Instruction; Online Campus Instruction; Building Professional Competence; Convenience of Time and Place; Adult-friendly Student Services; University's Faculty; Curricular Oversight; Teaching; Faculty Scholarship.

6. **Education in Globalising World** **213**
Globalisation and the Future of Education; Perceptions at the Beginning of the Century; The Context of Globalisation; Access to Information; Knowledge; Changes in the Labour Market, Diverse World Realities; Education in the New Context; Lifelong Learning for All; Distance Education and Distributed Learning; Institutionalisation of Networks.

7. **Future of Higher Education in Globalisation** **285**
Globalisation and the Universities; Mastering Globalisation; Importance of Higher Education; Systems of Higher Education; Governance; Science and Technology: The Importance of General Education; Implementation.

Bibliography 308

Index 310

Preface

Education is undergoing constant changes under the effects of globalisation. The introduction of information technology and communication is changing the delivery of education, changing the roles of students and teachers, and producing a shift in society from industrialisation towards an information-based society. The changes in education due to globalisation have also had profound effects upon a broad spectrum of cultures leading to suggestions of a new form of cultural imperialism. In addition, the structure of education is being altered to enable it to compete on an open, global market, leading to the 'commodification' of education.

Today, education is becoming a lifelong learning and training process, developing transferable skills and knowledge that can be applied to competitive markets where knowledge and information is being traded as a commodity. Globalisation is creating a fast paced, competitive environment through technology and communication which education systems must keep up with. Educational institutions around the world are being forced to compete globally, by engaging in entrepreneurial activities to sustain themselves in an uncertain and competitive world.

The rise of a global society, driven by technology and communication developments are shaping children, the future citizens of the world into 'global citizens', intelligent people with a broad range of skills and knowledge to apply to a competitive, information based society. The future of countries often lies within their ability to compete in a global market where industrial based economies are giving way to knowledge based industries, realising the importance of "knowledge, skills and the intellectual capacity to meet the challenges of accelerated change and uncertainty".

Editor

1

Education: Evolutionary Concept

The primary advantage of the work performed by those in charge of internationalization policies in universities and internationalization promoters is to be found in a field of activity which, while not allergic to criticism, is deemed to be beyond reproach. University internationalization is essentially centred on the international mobility of students and thus can hardly be blamed for promoting programs that allow students to reach out and better understand one another and to acquire international and intercultural skills. In the end, these programs sensitize students to the reality of global interdependence and global issues and, in doing so, groom them to become global actors who will have their say in how tomorrow's world will be configured. Given such a program, the only criticisms that can be made relate to the choice of the best means to increase the number of students travelling the international circuit, the implementation of safety and risk management measures, and the proposed pre-departure briefings and post-travel debriefings.

Thus, one of the essential components of the cultural universe of university internationalization practitioners is how to improve student and professor mobility and give this its true meaning in today's world. The other aspect of international university action obviously involves the internationalization of education itself. This means either redefining curriculum through the compulsory insertion of an international component or through the international networking of courses of study.

Knowledge today has become so diversified that it is no longer possible for a serious academic unit to claim that it can cover all components of a specific field of study and offer its students all areas of micro-specialization found in a given area of knowledge. Seen from this perspective, the international networking of programs, whether in the form of mutual agreements, joint programs, or double diploma arrangements, may consolidate and even enhance student training while facilitating the acquisition of the international and intercultural skills needed by today's young women and men. On the one hand, we can round out this scenario with sustained efforts to recruit foreign students whose considerable presence on campus both ensures a university's international reputation and internationalizes the campus itself.

On the other, we can implement research strategies that extend beyond the mere international publication of research results, integrating them into networks of international creators of new knowledge. We may then easily claim that the overall results of university internationalization are quite positive and henceforth play an increasingly important role in carrying out the mission of our institutions.

It is therefore understandable that university internationalization is acclaimed by many and, as we stated earlier, is seldom criticized. Indeed, what harm is there in doing good, that is, in graduating students who, in addition to receiving well-rounded academic training, have acquired international skills, opening a window to the outside world. Yet we must also ask ourselves if these university strategies for internationalization are sufficient and appropriate in the current context of development of knowledge-based societies, accelerating globalisation and greater mobility of human, financial, technological, cultural and social resources.

In other words, we hope that this article will provide an answer to the following question: Are we not witnessing a widening gap between the discourse and practices of internationalization, and the reality of the new issues facing the world of higher education? For many years, the field of international relations within political science crystallized the relationships existing between societies.

However, there are now grounds to believe that one major effect of the globalisation phenomenon has been to transform the relations between states into just one system among many other systems of relations created by other globalisation actors, be they business concerns, social movements, cultural organizations, institutions, etc. To sum up, if the interpretation of inter-state relations alone is no longer sufficient for understanding today's world, we must nonetheless admit that these relations are as important as ever. In fact, globalisation simply means a new space in which other social relations are organized and important dimensions of our lives in society are structured but it has not brought about the disappearance of international relations.

Namely, can a parallel be drawn between what university internationalization policies are to higher education and what international relations are to the globalised world in which we live? Do the internationalization policies of universities ignore the new issues raised by the globalisation of higher education?

The first term that comes to my mind is "intellectual monitoring." One of the most valuable contributions by academia to the life of our societies is that it constitutes one of the only social spaces in which a critical understanding of phenomena and the search for the truth can be conducted. In this sense, academia is first and foremost a space for dialogue that is essential to our societies and its contribution to the public sphere is unique owing to the quality and originality of the projects, analyses and research that are conducted there It should be noted, however, that any discussion on globalisation today is a delicate undertaking because the word itself has numerous meanings, including many negative connotations that would suggest that common sense has been blacklisted, judgement declared out of bounds and reason set aside. In a nutshell, it is an issue that polarizes reductive analyzes to extremes and while this is not an original solution; it can, despite everything, prove to be quite useful socially.

In the wake of events in Seattle in December 1999, Edgar Morin wrote in the French newspaper Le Monde that a second globalisation had been born, rooted in an awareness that control over globalisation can only be exercised globally. He went on to say that this movement associates a deep-rooted, cultural and civilized condition of sovereignty with a true awareness of world-wide problems, plus a renewed determination henceforth to take action for all those threatened by the hegemony of quantification, cost-effectiveness, profit-making and maximization.

A framework for thinking

From the outset, we must not underestimate the extent to which globalisation has upset the way we conceptualize reality, seriously casting doubt upon a collective concept based on the territorializing notion of our societies. This notion emphasizes the diachronic evolution of societies while relegating to secondary importance the variable spatial dimension, which is viewed as a given. This can be seen in our university curricula in the hegemony of history over geography in the analyses of our societies.

To summarize the process, this conceptualization, as it has evolved over more than a century of social sciences and humanities, is based upon well-known reflexes for understanding reality. Our usual way of understanding reality involves cutting it into national portions. In each portion we find a political community—a people, a nation-living on a territory separated from that of its neighbours by clearly defined borders. This community constructs and reproduces itself through its own internal dynamics. At the heart of this self-propelled construction is the State, an omnipresent architect of social order where it alone is empowered to legislate and enforce the law. The State acts as a modernizing force driving society because it is the most powerful organization and the only sovereign power over the territory. In our political science jargon, this is known as granting "primacy to domestic factors" since it is postulated that whatever occurs outside these national entities cannot be so important as to question the overall equilibrium that the State regulates within its territory.

Nonetheless, social sciences and political science in particular have not neglected the outside world. The division of labour within the discipline has seen the field of international relations take charge of studying the relationships and exchanges that these territorialized communities carry on amongst each other. Except that here, once again, the State is omnipresent in that the political universe made up of international relations is essentially structured by inter-state relations. All in all, our conceptualization is founded upon two central postulates that will summarize as follows:

> One, the territory as defined by the borders surrounding the State contains the life of the society; and, two, the relations that societies engage in are almost exclusively matters of State or, more accurately, inter-state relations rather than international relations.

Yet, each and every one of us, as ordinary citizens, know very well that our lives do not cease to exist at the borders of our society. Even citizens who do not frequently travel abroad will quickly recognize that the space in which they are evolving is plural and heterogeneous, and no longer coincides with the borders of the country where they live. The cultural, economic, educational, consumption, intellectual, religious, media, sports and social practices in their everyday lives are a part of social networks that do not share the same socio-spatial demarcation. These networks may be local, national, continental, occidental or even planetary or global.

You will note that among the practices listed above, those concerning the field of politics have been left out. This was purposely omitted since political practices, being spatially defined, are not of the same nature as the others. We may claim to be citizens of the world but we cannot get around the fact that our citizenship is specifically defined and restrictive. We are Canadian, American, French, Japanese, etc. and as such, the territory where we may exercise our political rights and responsibilities is clearly defined. Likewise, the territory over which the rules and regulations issued by the State apply is narrowly defined and generally the State' jurisdiction ceases at the borders that it has itsel established.

Basically, this theoretical conceptualization assumes on the one hand, a spatial correspondence between a the components of life in society, namely the economic cultural, social and political element, and on the other, territorialized concept of the community that insert individuals, groups and social classes into a clearl delimited societal framework, one which postulates tha the territory contains the life of the society.

In the world of higher education, this socia conceptualization is traditionally reflected in nationa university systems that contain university campuse which are territorialized premises. Thus, it is postulate that the campus contains the academic life since th professor remains the primary agent for teaching and th classroom, the main place for dispensing knowledge. On might think that in today's global world, this vision o the university is being put to task because, as Gérard Delanty has written: "Verbal communication is being challenged by new kinds of non-verbal communicatio and new kinds of agency. The producer and recipient of knowledge are no longer the professor and student engaged in scholarly discourse in the tutorial.

Knowledge is being depersonalized, deterritorialized and globalised. It is being taken out of its traditional context and disseminated by new media of communication. In the global age, the scholar's space is opening beyond the traditional spaces of the library, the seminar room and the study into a virtual level. The new technologies of communication have made feasible the virtual university. Whether this is the negation of the idea of the university or a new level of reality with which we have to live will be debated for some time..."

Why does the advent of globalisation upset this way of conceptualizing our societies and more specifically, the world of higher education? Essentially, because globalisation is a social process that radically redefines the space for any form of social action and where the compression of time shakes up our notions of the action's place and territory, thereby undermining their reality.

From my standpoint, this illustrious globalisation is structured by three factors. First, the loosening of the territorial attachment of the action, whether this be political, economic, educational, social, cultural, etc.; and, second, the creation of a new global space within which new global issues crystallize. The third and last factor is the role of this new space as the new forum for the confrontation and negotiation of collective preferences whose mission is to define this new global space. Expressed differently, globalisation is first and foremost an entire redefinition by the actors of their space for taking action. This quest obviously does not take place in a social vacuum. It is characterized by the emergence of new issues and the implementation of new rules and standards that will provide this global space with an orderly structure. To use the words of the Italian novelist, Alessandro Barricco, globalisation "is not only an extension of the playing field, it also involves changing the rules of the game. The globalized world is one that can only be built by eliminating a non-negligible portion of the rules respected until now.". Stated in this manner, globalisation is not to be understood as a mere continuation of internationalization.

Internationalization takes into account the state of exchanges and flows that occur between dispersed entities; for instance, the foreign trade between two countries, or the exchanges of students and professors between universities. In Barricco's view, globalisation means the construction of a new space that involves the acceptance of the actors who may be on the scene, the issues that will be tackled and the rules that will govern their operations.

Two major social phenomena, or two major changes, have favoured its emergence. The first originates in the fact that our societies are now organized around knowledge production, having evolved from an industrial development mode into a communications development mode. The immediate consequence of such evolution is that industrial goods no longer constitute the driving force behind economic activity, while the creation of new knowledge products are defining the capacity for innovation in socio-economics. Because of this transition, knowledge has undergone a change in status and has become a commodity that is bought and sold, exported and imported like any other product. The impact this has on university communities is momentous.The key factor to bear in mind, however, is that in this knowledge-based society, universities have lost their monopoly over the production and distribution of knowledge. Moreover, the presence of other market players now enjoying this same production capacity is leading to new university-institution-business partnerships or strategic alliances.

Finally, this has also led to a restructuring of research activities in universities around initiatives that are directly transferable to and profitable in the marketplace, all at the expense of other research whose focus is more long-term and whose economic impact is therefore more remote. In other words, these transformations potentially herald the coming of a new modus operandi in university communities, creating new stresses and fragmentation, and these must be assessed and understood.

New information technologies and their accelerated development obviously constitute the second factor that has contributed to the development of globalisation in university communities. Universities will be forced into making basic decisions in the near future as a result of the impact of information and communication technologies (ICTs) on research and teaching activities, their deterritorialization as well as their networking, the emerging e-learning global market and the presence of new players on this scene, and the creation of virtual universities, all in the context of a North-South digital fracture (and even within developed societies).

Finally, these transformations, which are clothed in a reductive, trickle-down discourse on globalisation seeking to make the marketplace the organizational focus for all life in society, have contributed to the emergence of practices and a mercantile discourse in universities which proposes the conquest of the education market as the only viable strategy. Furthermore, it is not unthinkable that the current round of World Trade Organization negotiations dealing with the General Agreement on Trades in Services (GATS) and the creation of the Free Trade Area of the Americas (FTAA), including removal of tariff barriers in the world of education, is a major issue that points to the direction of this mercantilization of higher education. We will have more to say about this further on.

These transitions are such that while they make globalisation more imposing, they also create new critical issues for universities. The first one involves the knowledge gap between universities in developed countries and those in emerging countries which has been widening continuously since the early 1980s. The past twenty years have seen an increase in the number of students attending universities world-wide but also widening gaps between the percentages of young people studying in emerging countries versus those in developed countries.

In addition, while there was one doctoral graduate per 5,000 inhabitants in OECD countries in 1997, there was only one per 70,000 in Brazil, one per 140,000 in Chile and one per 770,000 in Columbia. In a world dominated by new knowledge production, such statistics understandably become a source of concern regarding the possibility of emerging countries to successfully integrate into this new economy. The second major issue in the world of higher education is the brain drain from emerging countries to developed countries, an issue that university authorities will soon have to confront. The global demographic context, indicating relatively aging developed societies compared with very young emerging societies cannot by itself explain and justify this situation. Brainpower and expertise are the raw materials that nurture the knowledge-based economy. Stated rather bluntly, we must ask ourselves if after having guaranteed the growth of developed countries following World War II by what some have called the plundering of natural resources in countries of the South, will developed countries now in the early 21 st century go south once again to loot these countries of their intellectual elite? The relevance of this question can be seen in one example alone: only one-third of the 500,000 foreign students who annually attend an American university return to their country of origin. The brain drain issue raises highly critical questions of ethical and social import.

— It relates directly to the question of the collective needs of societies, whether emerging or developed, versus the development of individuals. This then points to the question of freedom of choice in a labour market of university graduates, which is itself specifically globalized.

— The brain drain raises the question of the relationship between university systems in emerging countries and those in developed countries. This is especially true since, as we have seen, there is a significant gap between emerging and developed countries in terms of accessibility to university studies and the fragility of graduate studies in certain southern countries, combined with aggressive recruitment of master's and doctoral students by universities in developed countries. Once again, we must ask ourselves if, in such a context, universities in the South are not just supplying skills to fill our graduate program quotas without receiving anything in return.

In other words, are emerging countries subsidizing graduate study programs in developed countries by providing them with the pick of their student crop without them having to pay the cost of their initial undergraduate training?

Regulating the global space of higher education?

These first two global issues raise a third one involving the means for regulating the global space of higher education that must be set in place. While knowledge and science are universal, university systems and the organization of university life are regulated by national policies and standards covering, to name just a few: financing, program accreditation, diploma recognition, and also student financing. The entire problem resides in the relationships between these national systems in regulating higher education while dealing with the global issues discussed earlier. Do these global issues exceed the level of competence of nation-states and do they require the implementation of a world-wide regulation of higher education that would ensure more equitable access to university studies and define models for new relationships in the world of higher education and the interactions between universities?

In other words, we are raising the question of an institutional deficit in the global space of higher education. As in other sectors of activity, such as international law or perhaps the environment, must we contemplate the creation of an "international or global plan" for higher education? Might we not find, in the construction of the European university space, lessons to be learned that could prove useful in the designing of a global institutional architecture?

If globalisation in no way lends itself to being reduced to its sole economic dimension and even less to that of a neo-liberal project, this must not blind us to the hegemony of the so-called neo-liberal project in the organization of new global spaces.

Contrary to what a quick analysis of the globalisation situation may lead one to believe, when faced with the question "What to do" regarding globalisation, more than one answer comes to mind. As regards higher education, it should be noted that there are also highly diversified proposals as to the organization and operating principles underlying this global university space. To begin with, there is a serious trend towards the commercialization and privatization of higher education via the importing of an entrepreneurial management and culture into the universities themselves, but also through the appearance of new private entrepreneurs who, under the university label, are offering educational products on the world market of higher education.

This observation cannot be sidestepped: the spatial restructuring of university actions is accompanied by a market culture that has university institutions exporting knowledge, selling or marketing their expertise, opening campus subsidiaries abroad, developing market opportunity strategies for winning over foreign students, reducing students to the status of client, all within a more general context of reducing tariff barriers and a significant reduction in the State's participation in financing universities. Authors such as Slaughter and Leslie conclude that this commercialization-privatization of universities is part of an even more important structural phenomenon which is the implementation of academic capitalism.

Others, myself included, are truly convinced of the failings of this project for commercializing higher education and thus are proposing that the global space encompassing university communities be structured around the notion of globally shared property. The negotiation of the very definition of this concept, its financing, choice of priorities and ways and means for collective actions, co-ordinating public and private actors, all raise even more critical and highly challenging issues involving the re-legitimization of international public intervention and the need for going beyond the current intergovernmental framework.

The enshrinement of higher education in a global project for sustainable human development that would answer the needs of present generations without compromising the capacities of future generations, or even the conception of universities as central vectors for the interconnections between societies also constitute other proposals for organizing this global space.

Obviously, we must draw up the widest range of possibilities for the organizational modelling of the global space occupied by higher education. Nonetheless, this short and non-exhaustive list that has been presented here demonstrates that the debate is now open and that the idea of structuring global space beyond the nation-state-implementing a suitable institutional architecture that will make it possible to democratically define all the processes for decision-making, assessing and legitimizing collective choices within the global space of higher education-quite likely constitutes the most important impact of globalisation on academia. In other words, we organized this conference based on the hypothesis that the debate on the impact of globalisation on higher education needs to be enriched and should not be reduced to a standoff between, on the one hand, partisans of hardline liberalism who preach market hegemony only to come to a dead end when faced with its democratic deficit and, on the other, those with a nostalgic ahistorical and asociological vision in which the university's mission needs no rethinking or updating and for whom globalisation is merely a threat from which higher education must be protected.

This is the most important impact of globalisation on universities: this order that beckons us to rethink the world of higher education and make universities participate in building a democratic and equitable world to live in. In so doing, it is possible that the gulf between the reality of academia and the debates that it seeks to promote on its own role might become that much smaller.

International Cooperation in Higher Education and Training

EU supports a wide range of smaller education and training programmes which, while having been initiated on the grounds of geopolitical and economic considerations, are at heart genuine educational cooperation activities. The question now poses itself how these relate to the accumulated experience of educational cooperation at large, to the state of the art in international cooperation. Given the fact that the majority of the previously mentioned programmes of cooperation with non-member states concern higher education and that it is also at the level of higher education that most experience in international educational cooperation has accrued, we decided that focussing on the higher education sector in our survey of the state of the art in international cooperation would be most constructive. By giving such an overview of the accumulated experience and progress in internationalisation at the level higher education we hope to be able to put existing schemes with non-member states into perspective. Once such a vista of the state of the art emerges, one will have to ask whether the definition, scope, target groups and organisational features of the current cooperation schemes are justified and offer the added value which one would want such schemes to achieve.

Globalisation, Internationalisation and Europeanisation

The rhetoric of higher education has always stressed internationalism. After the decay of a 'universal' church and its notion of a supra-national authority in the Renaissance, most universities were in fact founded by states to serve national interests. With the beginning of the new millennium, however, such national definitions are increasingly under attack or simply dissolve under pressures of growing competition and globalisation. Suddenly, universities are supposed to serve not just as "custodians of the genius of nations" but also "active instruments of national competitiveness". With the technological advances of transportation and information, scholarly and scientific contacts have multiplied and intensified. Students and information can travel quickly and cheaply between countries. Furthermore, after decades of efforts of internationalisation by idealistic individuals and progressive institutions, internationalisation has now become a key entrepreneurial arena in some countries, international student flows are being marketed, knowledge, in the form of skilled human resources, science, technology, research products, has become a vital resource for industrialised countries.

When talking about international cooperation, the term internationalisation often appears as a synonym for international cooperation. In light of the many different reflected and non-reflected uses of the terms internationalisation, globalisation and Europeanisation, our first step has to consist in some terminological clarifications. In the simplest sense, internationalisation refers to the sum of all those activities which aim to expand their reach over national borders. The process of integrating the international dimension into teaching, research and service functions of an institution of higher education, an international dimension referring to a perspective, activity or programme which introduces or integrates an international, intercultural or global outlook into the major functions of the institution. Another more selective understanding of the term emphasises "the process of systematic integration of an international dimension into the teaching, research and public service function of a higher education institution". In this sense, not many institutions which are active in international cooperation could be said to engage in internationalisation although, as we will point out later, a trend towards such systematic integration of an international dimension activities is clearly observable.

Globalisation refers to "forceful changes in the economic, social, political and cultural environment" brought about by global competition, the integration of markets, increasingly dense communication networks, information flows and mobility. Reflecting processes of global competitiveness, for example between great regional blocs such as the United States, the European Union and the Pacific Rim, implies, as Peter Scott formulates, a radical reordering of the old world-order of Great Powers since "national boundaries are rendered obsolete by the transgressive tendencies of high technology and mass culture".

Globalisation should not be confused with or simply regarded as a higher form of internationalisation for three reasons: while internationalisation presupposes the notion of nation states and is often conditioned by geo-political concerns, globalisation ignores or transcends the order of nation states altogether. Secondly, internationalisation processes are often owned, initiated and expressed by the "'high' worlds of diplomacy and culture" while globalisation belongs to the "'low' worlds of mass consumerism and global capitalism". Thirdly, depending on the unequal pattern of nation states, internationalisation tends to reproduce hierarchy and hegemony while globalisation processes can bring up new agendas beyond existing hierarchies.

Globalisation poses a fundamental challenge to tertiary education both with respect to the core functions of the university and to its institutional self-definition. For the purposes of our study, we see globalisation as the uncontrollable processes of dissolving national boundaries and hegemony brought about by world competition and the integration of markets both of which have been made possible by high technology. In contrast, internationalisation we regard as the active response of a given institution of higher education to the perceived insufficiencies of national definitions of the core functions of higher education. Since globalisation processes have often sharpened the perception of such insufficiencies among university representatives, internationalisation activities can in many cases even be regarded as institutional responses to globalisation processes. But while the latter ignore national boundaries, internationalisation works with them in order to transcend them.

Europeanisation, in the context of this study, we will simply regard as a geographical subset of internationalisation. In spite of the different political aims which are associated with its funding and the complex processes of regional integration and redistribution of power implied in the term, it has been shown that in most cases, the aims and handling of European cooperation activities at institutional level do not differ significantly from the rest of international cooperation activities and can be seen to contribute to internationalisation at large. Ironically, as the European Union, while talking about Europe, is a powerful actor of internationalisation, whereby Europe is actually predominantly a sub-category of less than systematic relevance.

Key Themes and Trends in the Current Debate on International Cooperation in Higher Education

International academic mobility

Student mobility

The best known form of internationalisation certainly is the increasing mobility of students studying abroad. Travelling students are of course a very old phenomenon and certain regions of the world have a long experience with it. Most European countries have known the influx of students from their former colonies. Large numbers of Latin American students seek to obtain postgraduate degrees in Northern American universities. In the heights of the Cold War the higher education institutions of the Soviet Union and Eastern European countries attracted students from ideologically associated nations. Furthermore, educational exchange between the US and Western Europe after 1945 was developed to foster democracy and develop the Atlantic community. Generally, geopolitical considerations always have been influential in policies regarding student mobility.

However, there is also a growing conviction that one of the most effective means to prepare future graduates for the needs of an increasingly international professional life in a global economy is simply to study and live abroad. The educational and social benefits, such as acquiring new and cross-cultural knowledge and competencies, improving foreign language proficiency (especially in English), establishing international personal and professional networks, becoming familiar with other countries and cultures, etc. are being stressed by international educators. In addition, broad cultural values such as internationalism in itself, the belief that cross-cultural educational and scientific exchange is a good in itself or that it promotes also the international understanding and cross-cultural sensitivity among home students and the wider community, go hand in hand with more economic considerations such as the broadening of educational markets and the generation of extra income.

Unlike the more marginal student mobility flows of earlier times, international student flows have now become a central feature of the global higher education system. Their quantitative development is impressive. Over the past forty years the world-wide growth rates in international student flows outweighed even the expansion rates of higher education in general, which underwent massification especially after the seventies. Recently, it seems that the number of foreign students in relative terms, i.e. measured as a percentage of the entire world student population, is actually on the decrease. This appears less surprising if one takes into account the massive expansion of higher education even on a global scale, which has now superseded the rise of foreign students. According to UNESCO statistics, there were some 1.5 million foreign students in the top 50 host countries in 1994-95. Over the last 25 years international student mobility has risen by more than 300%.

Most individual countries witness substantial growth rates of foreign student enrolment. Many observers expect its growth to continue for awhile, even if the annual growth rates will diminish gradually. Some prognoses make mention of 2.8 million students studying abroad world-wide by 2010 and 4.9 million by 2025, with the by far biggest expansion rates occurring in Asia from where 2.9 million students studying abroad are estimated to proceed in 2025. The imbalance of receiving and sending students seems to increase. As receiving countries the Anglo-Saxonhigher education systems attract by far the most significant shares. With respect to the mentioned exponentially increasing shares of students from Asia, for example, the USA alone receives nearly double as many students (291,000) as European countries do (170,500). In fact, Asian students constitute about well over half of all foreign students in the US. Of the share of Asian students hosted in the EU, about three fifths target the UK. Currently, about one third of the student mobility flows of the world are received by the US (nearly 500,000), a share which the president, secretary of state and the secretary of education of the United States are eager to augment. Australia has been greatly increasing its share of incoming students from abroad. In one decade the number of foreign students enrolled at Australian universities has tripled. Europe occupies a rather unusual position as compared with other industrialised countries: While Europe hosts about half of all foreign students (51%), more than half of these students also originate from other European countries.

While most discussions on internationalisation focus on organised student mobility in the framework of programmes, this in fact only represents about a fifth if not less of the overall student mobility flows. In Europe, where numbers in organised mobility are probably highest world-wide, the percentage of organised mobility probably does not exceed 20%. When talking about conditions of student mobility programmes we should keep this fact in mind, especially as we turn to the possible future courses of action which should take account of these less controllable more market-oriented flows. If we turn now to the small but significant share of international student mobility which is supported and stimulated by various kinds of programmes and schemes, it should be noted that most countries have a variety of bilateral and multilateral agreements and programmes in this field. One of the best known programmes of international student mobility is the European ERASMUS and subsequent SOCRATES programme. Started in 1987 with a view towards the common market of 1992,

ERASMUS had the ambition, among other goals, to increase significantly the mobility of students - 10% of the overall student population were targeted to have studied abroad at least once for a term, semester of year during their degree courses in order to develop the European dimension of higher education and to strengthen a European social identity. Such immersion in other European contexts was seen to support the creation of an internal market of professionals and qualified workers.

Since prior to Maastricht the European Commission had no explicit competencies in education and direct strategies at harmonisation of the structures of higher education were considered to be beyond its political competence, student mobility was the vehicle of a strategy of Europeanisation of higher education. Within less than ten years it reached the level of more than 100,000 mobile European students a year and with this result it was considered to be one of the most successful European programmes in the field of education, even if the original target of giving 10% of all EC-students the opportunity to study abroad was not reached. To some extent, the success of ERASMUS / SOCRATES is of course also due to supportive national policies of member states, providing additional funding. ERASMUS and SOCRATES are not the sole, perhaps not even the most important frameworks of international student mobility in the world. In the Asia/Pacific region the "University Mobility in Asia and the Pacific" programme (UMAP), established in 1991, is important although it has not yet resulted in some kind of funding scheme. Smaller student mobility programmes exist in most world regions. International student mobility increasingly is a regional and not only an intercontinental phenomenon. Regional economic integration processes also instigate student mobility and international treaties such as NAFTA, ASEAN or APEC have proven to be stimulating in this respect. Changes in development aid policies also tend to stress more regional student mobility than South-North mobility.

The ERASMUS / SOCRATES programme in Europe and the UMAP in the Asia-Pacific region are specifically designed to promote regional student mobility. Of regional nature is also the NORDPLUS-programme of student exchange in the Nordic countries with its original and attractive "money follows student"-imperative. Besides this more or less organised mobility there is also an important "spontaneous" mobility of "free movers", taking place outside schemes and programmes. As Todd Davis has shown for the US and Gordon and Jallade for the European situation, this spontaneous mobility can be attributed to a mixture of "push" and "pull" factors, such as national differences in access (numerus clausus regulations in certain disciplines) on the one hand and language and cultural considerations and the perceived quality differentials on the other hand.

The most important global movement still is that towards the United States, which is the largest receiving country of foreign students with 34% of the OECD-total (OECD, 1997). The transatlantic mobility between Europe (and other world regions) and the US for example, implemented on a multilateral and reciprocal basis under the International Student Exchange Program (ISEP), is confronted with an increasing unbalance. American universities have a growing attraction on European students and the growth of intra-European programmes has not negatively affected this, while European universities seem to have lost some of their attractiveness for US-students. The world-famous top research universities of the US exert an enormous attraction on mobile students all over the world, but also the second rank American universities receive important numbers of foreign students. The dominance of English as the lingua franca in contemporary science and scientific training and the most commonly mastered second language contributes to the fact that besides the US also the UK, Canada and Australia are among the top host countries world-wide. From the point of view of the countries of origin of mobile students, it is clear that market-driven, economic factors put into the shade older, more traditional links such as (post) colonial relations. It is no wonder that the newly industrialising economies of the Asian and Pacific region are major sources of foreign students, who aspire to fill the ranks of the growing professional classes.

The example of Australia shows that the emergence of a more trade-oriented policy towards foreign students, whereby universities engaged in student recruitment and marketing strategies, was a fruitful enterprise at least from a mercantile point of view. Education is seen by the Australian state as the fastest growing export industry, which was expected to generate an export income of 3.5 billion US$ by the year 2000, hopes which were put on hold due to the Asian-Pacific economic crisis. The number of full-fee paying international student enrolment rose from 7,131 in 1987 to more than 143,000 full-fee-paying students in 1996 in Australia, including 54,000 at the higher education level.

Indeed, international student flows have become "more trade than aid" in many host countries, since often international students are or have become full-fee-paying students. In many host institutions, especially in Anglo-Saxon countries, the income of fee-paying foreign students is a welcome addition to shrinking domestic funding, without which many departments would be threatened with closure. Revenue generation has become an important rationale in institutional policies promoting recruitment of foreign students.

A growing part of international student mobility thus is becoming market-driven rather than state-driven or aid-oriented. The international market in education services is becoming a booming sector and the international marketing of domestic universities and the recruitment of students are central elements of it. Some countries are developing well-organised national policies in this field, such as France with its marketing initiative by EduFrance and its 1,058 associations in 132 countries of the Alliance Française, or Great Britain with the "Welcome to the UK" initiative and the British Council's 211 offices in 147 countries.

Some countries, such as Canada, Australia, New Zealand and even South Africa after 1994, have developed ambitious strategic plans in order to strengthen their market position in the field. With the end of the strong expansion at universities, which, after decades of massive expansion, had seemed to most higher education representatives like a kind of "natural" growth, the opposite trend is already being observed in some fields and many countries, namely a growing trend to seek and actively compete for students, also for the sake of maintaining sufficient levels of public funding which is linked to student enrolment in most countries. In many higher education communities this is something new, which also induces many actors to try and discover new "markets" of potential students. Since one may expect students' choices to increase, institutions of higher education will have to and are beginning to pay more attention to their needs and satisfaction than was customary e.g. in continental Europe in the past.

Academic Staff Mobility

Although not as extensively researched as student mobility, staff mobility can be considered the second most important form of internationalisation in higher education. The distinction line with student mobility is not always very clear due to the large numbers of mobile postgraduate and Ph.D. students. In many regions and specific areas of study, such as business administration, regional and international training networks for young researchers and professionals have become well-established. Of course, there is a great deal of "natural" mobility in the academic profession, due to the international character of scientific research and training.

Traditionally, international mobility among professors is most often motivated by research and scholarship and is stimulated by the growth of global and increasingly competitive research scenes with its abundant conferences, meetings and joint research projects, but also by the availability of cheap air travel. Education and teaching have become reasons for international mobility only recently. As with student mobility there is a great deal of geographic inequality in the mobility flows.

The International Survey of the Academic Profession has shown a high polarisation between countries with high academic immigration, sometimes as a result of deliberate international recruitment of academic staff for expanding higher education systems (e.g. Hong Kong), and countries with low levels of internationalisation of faculty. The latter are mostly countries which are either more ethnically homogeneous, do not use English as a language of instruction or have a small range of countries to draw upon for academics speaking their own language.

The US and the UK are the major important ex- and importers of academic labour, but compared to the domestic production of highly skilled academics the picture is much more diverse. Developing countries and Eastern European countries face the problem of emigration of researchers and academic staff to the global centres of research. A massive problem of brain drain therefore exists on a global scale at the expense of developing and "second world" regions. Especially Africa faces a huge problem of academic brain drain, caused by political instability and slow social-economic recovery.

Mobility of professors and scientists seems to have encouraged the emergence of a global marketplace in scientists, rather than to have advanced the internationalisation of higher education at a global scale. Programmes such as ERASMUS/SOCRATES and UMAP promote regional teaching staff mobility projects alongside student mobility. Some bilateral programmes, such as Fulbright, also focus on staff mobility. In ERASMUS/SOCRATES, staff exchanges are promoted as part of a more or less regular cooperation between European higher education institutions. Teichler rightly denotes that for the European Commission teaching staff mobility was not an end it itself but an instrument which formed part of the more general aim to denationalise curricula and to develop European courses by developing inter-institutional networks. However, most of the mobility of academic staff within ERASMUS projects is for relatively short periods. Many travelling professors point to problems associated with the heavy teaching load in their home universities and with limited financial and administrative support for teaching abroad. It is clear that within ERASMUS before and with SOCRATES, where it gained a greater emphasis within the framework of the "institutional contract", teaching staff mobility has still not received a decisive push, neither from the funding agencies nor from the institutions of higher education.

Internationalising Curricula

The notion of a growing interdependence of national economies and labour markets has become established enough to spread the view that human resources should also be qualified to act successfully on an international stage. Accordingly, more and more representatives of the labour markets and higher education institutions see the need to integrate foreign languages and courses on foreign cultures, politics and legal frameworks into existing curricula. Furthermore, the political integration process in the European Union has fostered the desire to support the construction of a European citizenship and social identity with European studies elements in relevant disciplines, in addition to the additional knowledge of the framework conditions of a European labour market.

However, the respect of the variety of national systems of higher education and the subsidiary powers of governments and institutions with regard to curricula has often dampened the aspiration to de-nationalise curricula. In Europe, the de-nationalisation of curricula was viewed with such mistrust - especially by member state authorities who feared that their competence was being encroached upon—that the introduction of European elements into existing curricula could only be realised by means of mobility projects. This was one of the reasons why the management of mobility programmes was situated at the level of the departments and not, as in the American examples, at the level of the institutions and their central international offices.

Nevertheless, ERASMUS cooperation and the Commission's support is seen by its most well-known evaluator, Teichler, to have contributed significantly to the de-nationalisation of higher education curricula, be it through the obligation to recognise study abroad for the home degrees and thereby the need to compare curricula, or through the support of actual joint curriculum development in the context of inter-departmental partnerships (ICPs). Teichler even states that "the Commission's contribution to internationalisation rests primarily on its successful challenge to national forces of curricular coordination. It is clear, however, that the new emphasis of the "Europeanisation" of curricula under ERASMUS/SOCRATES has been received with great restraint and caution, mainly due to the limited funding available". Strategic attempts initiated "from above" and aimed at the internationalisation of curricula have not always been very successful, neither in Europe nor abroad. Mestenhauser calls the internationalisation of curricula the "sacred cow" and refers to Woodrow

Wilson's saying as president of Princeton University that "it is easier to move cemeteries than to change the curriculum".

Nevertheless, there are some meaningful developments towards international curricula in various countries and regions. Van der Wende has researched several of these developments comparatively. She used the rather broad OECD-typology of international curricula ranging from curricula with some international content, over curricula that address cross-cultural skills, to curricula leading to internationally recognised professions and special curricula designed for foreign students. She witnessed a strong and recent increase in the number of internationalised curricula in several of the researched countries, although the picture is very diffuse in these countries.

Most of these international curricula are found in the areas of economics and business studies, the humanities and social sciences. Van der Wende also notes that the joint development, delivery and certification (joint or double/triple degrees) of programmes are more widely found in the European Union than in the Asian-Pacific region. From her international comparative analysis some conditions for successful development and successful implementation emerged which were acknowledged across the various countries analysed and could therefore be considered as internationally valid. These conditions for success include sufficient institutional autonomy, sufficient flexibility in curriculum regulations within the institution, internationalising the curriculum being regarded as an academic challenge to staff, broad involvement and commitment of staff, a senior academic moderating the process, endorsement from top management, consistency with the institutional mission and policy, combined top-down and bottom-up strategy, administrative support infrastructure and services for the reception of foreign students and staff, and, last not least, extra budgets.

Internationalising curricula can also be seen as something more comprehensive than developing curricula with international components, namely the international harmonisation of curricula. The most powerful inducement to internationalise curricula has probably come from the growing impact of international professional associations. The rapid growth in international trade in professional services has provoked several professions to organise themselves at an international scale. These international professional associations started to deal with issues of education and training, such as quality assurance, international minimum standards, criteria of professionalism, accreditation, etc. and usually promote the greater convergence of curricula and quality criteria. Some professions have been very active in this matter, such as the engineering, the medical or the legal professions. Professional associations, organised at an international level, thus have exerted a harmonising influence on standards and curricula in view of the professional accreditation of programmes and the professional recognition of degrees in various countries.

In some instances, these international professional standards are legally enforced by international organisations. The European Union for example increasingly deals with minimum standards of education and training in view of the mobility of labour and the recognition of entry into specific professions in the common market. Also organisations such as OECD and WTO are becoming increasingly interested in these matters and free trade agreements such as NAFTA or ASEAN often contain clauses on mutual recognition of licensing or certification procedures in view of the international mobility of professional services. But also from the point of view of removing mobility obstacles, the motivation to render curricular structures more homogeneous has grown significantly in many countries, especially in the EU in recent years.

After years of member state resistance to curricular homogenisation, the impulse to at least obtain a comparable curricular structure in Europe has now come from the national governments. With the declarations of Sorbonne and Bologna, the signatory member state and other governments commit themselves to converging reforms in the curricular architecture which are likely to set off a major surge of new curriculum development motivated by the aim of international compatibility and accessibility.

Recognition and Transparency

The main thrust of the past decades of international cooperation in higher education has been on cooperation and exchanges within existing structures, made possible by efforts to create some degree of transparency between very different national systems. The recognition of degrees or diplomas obtained in a foreign country back at the home institution or labour market has been a preoccupation of international organisations and the focus of a number of declarations, conventions and agreements between states for several decades.

Information centres and electronic databases have been established in order to obtain some degree of transparency regarding foreign curricular, degree and grading structures. The most impressive development in this field has taken place in the European Union. Already in the fifties the Council of Europe has set up conventions and information centre networks in order to enhance mobility in Europe.

Together with the UNESCO's centre for higher education (CEPES) an important "Convention on the recognition of qualifications concerning higher education in the European region" was adopted in Lisbon in April 1997. Here it is no longer assumed that there are strict standards of equivalence. Instead the existing diversity of systems of education and ongoing diversification of higher education is acknowledged by the emphasis of the concept of recognition and the trust upon the effectiveness of the other countries' systems of quality assurance and accreditation.

An important information tool was also promoted through the convention, the so-called "Diploma Supplement", which was developed by UNESCO, the Council of Europe and the European Commission. While it had been on the political agenda since the mid-1980s, it was now adopted as an instrument to improve the possibilities for diploma recognition by describing given national diplomas in type, level, contents and status, thus allowing for a level of transparency which is supposed to lead to a de facto recognition of foreign degrees in European countries.

The national information centres (ENIC) are also supposed to facilitate recognition procedures at national level. With a similar purpose but in a separate network of centres, the National Academic Recognition Information Centres (NARIC) were set up with the support of the European Union. In this context, the ERASMUS programme should be mentioned again since it was the first funding instrument world-wide which obliged institutions to fully recognise periods studied and credits earned abroad. While this obligation was not always observed very diligently in the early years of ERASMUS, pressure has increased on institutions to implement this guideline.

In order to support institutions in their efforts to grant recognition, the EU developed a separate instrument, the European Credit Transfer System (ECTS). This system, which constitutes another important tool to enhance transparency across borders, was developed and tested between 1989 and 1995 during a pilot project involving 145 European higher education institutions which refined and prepared the system for wider use. Consisting of a 'learning agreement' between student, host and home institution, an information package on the host institution describing the content and relative weight of each course in the curriculum, and a transcript of records, ECTS is an attempt to quantify periods and components of study and thus to facilitate their transferability. With the introduction of ECTS as an activity fundable under ERASMUS/SOCRATES which even received great rhetorical emphasis with the introduction of the institutional contract under SOCRATES, ECTS has quickly extended its scope and now is being introduced at the majority of institutions in the EU, with attempts to apply it in a modified form even for student mobility between Europe and non-European countries.

Of course, ECTS lends itself more easily to higher education systems which are based on credit accumulation systems. But it now seems to have exerted considerable pressure on non-credit systems to adapt. In the framework of SOCRATES, with its emphasis on new cooperation activities and the introduction of the institutional contract, ECTS has been given more scope at most institutions. However, ECTS is not intended as a solution to problems of equivalence of courses and credits as far as contents or quality goes, even though it is often misunderstood as such. It is a quality-neutral translation tool, which is effective only if it is not over-rated in its use.

Beyond the simple translatability of diverse course offerings, there have been even some signs lately of growing acceptability of harmonisation of curricular structures because of numerous practical and logistic problems in international mobility programmes. Issues such as the structuring of the academic year or the size of credits and modules increasingly are seen as susceptible for international harmonisation which was formerly regarded as a taboo. Concerning the far more important issue of the structure of an academic programme in an undergraduate and a graduate cycle, there is a slow evolution towards general acceptance of some Anglo-Saxon model. Stimulated by advocates of internationalisation in international businesses and structured professions, academics and policy makers tend to recognise the advantages of gradual harmonisation of the basic characteristics of university education.

The most ambitious developments in this respect are the Sorbonne and Bologna Declarations, which also focussed on the theme of the transparency and translatability of European systems of education. Both are inter-governmental declarations and are based on joint efforts of ministers of education and higher education representatives. They aim at setting up gradually a common European space for higher education which is supposed to designate a common structure of degrees rather than a gradual homogenisation of contents. While the first, the Sorbonne Declaration was followed by a somewhat confused and concerned debate about its alleged recommendation of a single pattern of degrees after three, five, and eight years in higher education, which was perceived as a threat to Europe's cherished diversity, the Bologna Declaration, which was prepared by an exhaustive survey of Europe's jungle of degree structures and areas of convergence and divergence, sets up a work schedule and programme to achieve a European space of readable and comparable degrees, undergraduate and postgraduate, with a first degree no shorter than 3 years and clearly relevant to the labour market, ECTS-compatible credit systems everywhere, a European dimension in quality assurance and an improvement of the free movement of students and teachers through structural reforms in all 29 signatory countries.

Institutions of higher education are now challenged to introduce meaningful first degrees which are shorter, more flexible (through the adoption of credit systems), more relevant to professional life, more multidisciplinary, more European and international, as well as to create masters degrees in environments where there were no short, or separate, programmes at this level in order to meet the needs and expectations of the mobile students from the rest of Europe and the world.

The main benefit one would expect from the development of such independent master's courses would be to have a much wider redistribution of students entering the postgraduate level than we currently have, which could also pave the way for a new type of mobility. Most remarkably perhaps, the Bologna Declaration signals a political turning point in the history of cooperation in higher education since it constitutes a pledge freely taken by the 29 signatory countries to reform their own systems in such a way that its structures may converge clearly and thus constitutes a dramatic shift away from the generally hesitant and reactive role which the member states of the EU used to play in a political scene of university cooperation which was most often fuelled by initiatives of the European Commission.

Institutional and Strategic Integration of International Cooperation Activities

Increasingly, international education moves higher in institutional priorities and becomes a major concern of the central administration, in Europe as well as in other industrialised countries. In the US, the Association of International Education Administrators (AIEA), in cooperation with national academic associations, published very influential Guidelines for International Education at US Colleges and Universities already in 1983 which called for the establishment of one central institutional "lead point", a senior administrator with the responsibility "for developing strategy and managing activities tied to internationalising the institution." In Europe, the European Commission revised the managerial framework of its successful ERASMUS programme in 1994 in order to enhance institutional commitment and foster the central administration's involvement and support of European cooperation. Accordingly, ERASMUS/SOCRATES now requires that higher education institutions collect the whole array of European cooperation activities under the framework of one institutional application and formulate a "European Policy Statement" every three years explaining the status and context of their planned cooperation activities.

Only in a few European countries, such internationalisation statements were already established practice. The majority of higher education institutions formulated such a policy statement for the first time and did not just adapt an already existing policy statement for the purpose. As recent studies have shown, these new requirements have indeed contributed to lending greater visibility and transparency to internationalisation issues and practice in the eyes of the central administration and decision-making bodies, leading in many cases to increased support and coordination of exchange services, institution-wide recognition guidelines and mobilisation of hitherto inactive areas.

It is generally agreed that it makes a great difference whether the initiative for internationalisation proceeds from a component of the institution, such as a department or research group, or whether the institution's internationalisation is also being initiated, coordinated, planned and systematically integrated by the institution's central leadership. Of course, institutional contexts in which international cooperation activities are being undertaken vary greatly. A seminal model describing the variation of institutional internationalisation processes has been developed by

Davies. He differentiates two dimensions: one proceeds from sporadic uncoordinated efforts of internationalisation to systematic and carefully planned ones; the other characterises the locus of international initiative in the institution as varying from marginal to central. Thus Davies presents a matrix according to which an institution can have

— a systematic-central organisation type where "there is a large volume of international work in many categories, which reinforce each other and have intellectual coherence. The international mission is explicit and followed through with specific policies and supporting procedures";

— an ad hoc-central organisation type where a high level of activity may take place throughout the institution but is not based on clear concepts, coordination, prioritisation and has therefore an ad hoc character;

— a systematic-marginal organisation type where the level of activities is limited but these are well-coordinated, prioritised and based on clear planning and decisions;

— an ad hoc-marginal organisation type where little activity takes place and the activities are not based on clear decisions.

The "institutionalisation" of the whole variety of international cooperation activities would thus signal progress as compared to the more anarchic state of many unrelated cooperation activities co-existing in an institution without awareness of each other. Interestingly, as van der Wende points out, innovation theory also regards institutionalisation as the last stage which decides the ultimate fate of an idea for change. Referring to Levine's work on innovation in higher education, she highlights institutionalisation as the most critical phase for any innovation. Levine's own research shows that innovations are usually transformed or die during the "institutionalisation - termination phase". The most positive outcome of an innovation in this phase would be if its characteristics were allowed to spread through the host organisation ("diffusion").

Many higher education institutions are currently moving into this crucial phase of institutionalisation, often helped or propelled into it by support from funding schemes. A good case in point is the ERASMUS programme and its new requirements under the SOCRATES framework. While the early phase of ERASMUS had been characterised by a pioneer spirit of persons who decided to devote time and energy to make the innovation a success, ERASMUS under SOCRATES tried to address questions about the need for continuity and reliability of cooperation activities independent of the coincidental strengths and weaknesses of the pioneers.

The move from initial ERASMUS to ERASMUS under SOCRATES - with its requirement to describe the institutional context and underlying policy motivating the planned activities and apply for all of the cooperation activities within one framework application - may be regarded as the most visible support measure accompanying the transition from casuistic to systematic treatment of the international dimension in higher education. The institutions were suddenly challenged not to consider their international activities any more as marginal, non-coherent, decentralised activities of individuals but rather as important, costly activities which require a certain stability as well as a common in frastructural support if they were to lead to cross-fertilisation, activities which are supposed to be relevant to the quality and reputation of the institution as a whole.

Interestingly, analyses of the 1,600 Policy Statements submitted to the European Commission as part of the Institutional Application and case studies of the processes of preparation and implementation of the policy statements revealed that institutions appreciated the occasion to gather an overview of all of their international cooperation activities and to mobilise hitherto inactive areas but, in a vast majority of cases, were reluctant to introduce highly interventionist strategic action or to shift their emphases away from student mobility, which continued to be the core of most institutional European policies.

Nevertheless, SOCRATES can be said to have pushed those institutions which had a very casuistic approach towards internationalisation to make the latter a regular topic of discussion and coordination, to have led to the creation of mechanisms for reflection, information and transparency regarding the level and content of the institution's cooperation activities, as well as to have systematised decision-making regarding international issues from the pioneers' coincidental decisions to the general decision-maker to regular policy. Teichler inserts his description of the institutional responses to the changes of the ERASMUS programme requirements into a general model which also implies a natural evolution from "casuistic" to "systematic" approaches as internationalisation activities expand:

Regarding strategic development, Teichler predicts that by virtue of the fact that internationalisation will tend to "more and more affect the whole life of the institution of higher education, the major consequence might not be so much the prioritisation of strategic options, but rather care that this dimension is taken seriously across the board in all major activities". Many institutions opted for systematic approaches and have therefore changed in three respects. In matters of management, they have established regular responsibilities and regular modes of decision-making procedures regarding international issues. For example, vice-presidents or pro-rectors have been assigned the task of coordinating international issues. Committees for international affairs have been set up or existing committees entrusted with the task on a regular basis. At faculty and/or departmental level, deans or other staff have been appointed to coordinate and help the implementation of internationalisation.

With respect to infrastructure and services, internationalisation clearly results in the expansion of services, be they related to foreign language training, accommodation for foreign students or scholars, information and administrative support, counselling or other functions. Accordingly, many institutions have extended their international offices or established such offices if they did not exist before. At most institutions, international offices play the double role of providing services for regular international activities and of preparing and administering the international policies of the institution.

The extension of the role and influence of the international relations administration and offices has been noted to lead to an increasing professionalisation of international education administrators in Europe as well as in the United States where national norms have even been developed with respect to professional administration of student mobility and elsewhere.

If institutionalisation of international cooperation activities is seen to be desirable mainly because of the sustainability and better synergies and cross-fertilisation between activities, it may be helpful at this point to recall the range of possible activities which serve to internationalise a given institution of higher education, in order to then think of the ways in which such activities can be institutionalised, i.e. integrated into the institution's mission, planning and review systems, policies and procedures, hiring and promotion systems. Knight presents two rather comprehensive lists of activities and mechanisms of institutionalisation under the labels "programme strategies" and "organisational strategies" which offer a useful overview over the realm of institutional options.

Explaining her first table, Knight observes that the first category of the first table is perhaps closest to what is generally considered internationalisation activities. The second category can touch upon the substantive nature of research, its methodology and the distribution of knowledge. The third category of external relations has traditionally been oriented to international development activities and bilateral cooperation agreements between institutions, it is gradually shifting to less of an "aid" and more of a "trade" focus, with commercial activities like the export of educational products and services increasing in scope. Networks between institutions also with the private sector are also increasing in importance so that this category may well be the one undergoing the swiftest change at the moment. The last category is often forgotten but should be remembered in view of bringing a comparative perspective to the campus and the classroom.

The dangers of top-heavy strategic management, which have recently been brought to the fore in the study of the implementation of SOCRATES where growing de-motivation and loss of ownership among academics active in ERASMUS have been observed, are often emphasised by the EAIE. The individual commitment a conditiosine qua non of internationalisation and inter-institutional cooperation: "This is clearly underlined by many inter-institutional linkages established between heads of institutions, without appointment of a responsible academic, which lead their life largely and are not followed by any cooperation activity".

Institutional Networking

Collaboration between universities is hardly new, but institutional forms of cooperation agreements dealing with various aspects of education and teaching constitute a rather recent phenomenon. They are often developed in the context of collaboration projects dealing with student and/or teaching staff exchange. For example, in the framework of ERASMUS-ICPs and even more formally in the case of the bilateral agreements which are supposed to underpin each "institutional contract" in SOCRATES, denser institutional relationships have been developing between European universities. In this context a deeper institutional engagement is implied in various forms of inter-institutional agreements which in one way or another seek to recognise the educational programmes of one institution to another. In most cases, international links have started as people-to-people relationships which might but need not result in interdepartmental or inter-faculty links and even in a formalised inter-institutional agreement at a later stage. For many years, until the introduction of the "Institutional Contract" under SOCRATES, the structural backbone of ERASMUS constituted a formalised collaboration between departments or faculties, misleadingly called "inter-university cooperation programme" - an organisational principle which was later also adopted by the UMAP programme.

While for any large-scale and systematised cooperation an enhanced degree of institutional commitment is a necessary complement to such departmental multilateral links, it has recently been quite clearly confirmed that no institution-based agreement and internationalisation strategy can live without the life-vein of these academic contacts. Recent studies of the implementation of SOCRATES showed that the programme's change of emphasis away from the multilateral transnational network structure to the institutional embedding of cooperation activities in central coordination and priority setting was only partly successful.

Numerous interviews with affected professors and administrators revealed that the down-side of the new managerial modus of the programme is widely regarded to be its lack of support to multilateral departmentally-based networks since these are felt to be the true motor and animator of academic cooperation. As it has been argued by programme representatives that, when it comes to concrete cooperation activity, multilaterality boils down to a sum of bilateralities, one may ask what it is about multilateral networking that can be regarded as vitally important. Typical answers by concerned academics point to several advantages of multilateral networking. They were seen to be:

— more efficient for solving problems with network partners than a series of bilateral meetings, especially regarding academic integration, comparison of teaching contents, not just because all network partners were present at one place at one time, but also because of the abundance of potential mediators;

— necessary for truly integrated teaching staff mobility, the preparation of which demands a lot of communication and which can be helped by other partners' experience;

— a good probing ground for possible joint curriculum development;

— an optimal opportunity to find new partners, helped by the mediation of established partners present (this was strongly voiced by newcomers to ERASMUS in the CEEC);.

— an excellent tool for building a European identity for all the partners involved - at multilateral meetings, national identities were seen to be feeding better into a common European group identity, better than any series of bilateral meetings could ever hope to achieve.

Other observers point to the opportunities for more structured and more sustainable cooperation as well as economies of scale, due to multilateral communication.

The pooling of expertise which such discipline-based or thematic multilateral networks bring about are also said to offer particularly fruitful soil for the growth of new ideas, new project plans, for innovation.

Some such interdepartmental partnerships have accumulated with such density between two institutions that true inter-university relationships may develop from them. If these in turn discover a common sense of purpose, context or institutional development, they may turn and have in a number of cases turned into inter-university networks. In such inter-institutional networks, institutions attempt to address each other as a whole and even as allied political actors in the European scene of higher education. Examples for such inter-institutional networks which try to form around a common sense of identity are the SANTANDER Group, the UTRECHT, UNICA or COIMBRA networks.

In most cases, the actual competencies of such networks in the field of education and teaching are rather limited. Rather than being networks in which very specific common approaches to education are developed and implemented, these networks are to be seen as rather loose fora for discussion and exchange of experience. However, some networks are actually evolving into more ambitious cooperative entities with common self-definitions and self-presentations and common lines of strategic development, which is also seen to serve their status and competitive advantages on the international market of higher education services.

The closest form of inter-institutional cooperation is represented by the mutual recognition of the educational programmes of two institutions - agreements which may lead to the establishment of important international university networks at a global scale. The "Global Alliance for Transnational Education" (GATE), an important international organisation of businesses, higher education institutions and governmental agencies in the field of quality assurance, accreditation and certification in international education, distinguishes different forms of such inter-institutional arrangements, namely "franchising", "twinning" and "articulation".

Under franchising agreements an institution grants a host institution in another country the permission to provide some of the courses and degrees of the first, under mutually agreed conditions; the education provided resorts completely under the degree-awarding capacity of the home institution while the host institution is responsible for the actual provision of the course offer. In twinning agreements, higher education institutions in different countries offer joint programmes where students follow exactly the same courses, have the same materials and pass the same examinations, although the academic staff is usually engaged locally. Contrary to twinning agreements, at "articulated" institutions students are enrolled in programmes or part of programmes in the host institution which lead to credits recognised by the other institution without the courses having been developed jointly.

The example of the networks mentioned above also shows how inter-university recognition agreements may sometimes be the first step toward the cooperating partners transforming themselves into a real transnational network of institutions. Current trends suggest that such networks will trade in the global educational marketplace in the future while the constituent parts may want to maintain their respective national identities. Such transnational networks are in a better position to develop a more internationally marketable image, by pooling their respective expertise and by building on their experience with intercultural and international communication and cooperation.

Another interesting development is the prospect of transnational mergers of institutions. A European attempt has been made in Limburg, where the Belgian (Flemish) "Limburgs Universitair Centrum" (LUC) and the Dutch "Universiteit Maastricht" are planning close forms of cooperation in the field of academic education, which are eventually to lead to a transnational merger. Such a development could result in important institutional benefits, since the new university could integrate its statutory educational supply and degree-awarding capacities and thus transgress national limitations in planning and programming. In many countries, national legislation in higher education is not prepared to deal effectively with real transnational institutions. Since all of the above-mentioned agreements and arrangements are made at an institutional level within the space of autonomy left to the educational market, they mostly remain unknown to the political authorities. Sometimes they may even transgress national procedures and frameworks of educational planning, recognition of diplomas, accreditation and quality assurance.

Internationalisation and Quality Assurance

In the past decade, the quality of educational provision has become an increasingly urgent concern in most countries. The growing urgency with which the issue of quality has been dealt with among higher education representatives but also among politicians and government officials and other stakeholders can be attributed to a number of factors. First of all, as van Damme points out, the massification of higher education has exerted increasing pressure on infrastructures as well as on human and financial resources and has heightened the need for efficient expenditure.

Secondly, key stakeholders, businesses, professional bodies and employer organisations have voiced their concern about the capacities of traditional academic management to guarantee adequate quality standards and to respond to the needs of modern work places and labour markets in an increasingly competitive and transformative economy. Thirdly, in most industrialised countries, budget restrictions and fiscal crises have led to a decrease in government funding per student and a pressure to increase efficiency in public expenditure. Fourthly, the deregulation of many national higher education system has not only increased institutional autonomy but also the demands of the "evaluative state" and public accountability.

The establishment of quality assurance policies and mechanisms in many countries took place in a political and governmental environment characterised by a changing relationship between the state and the institutional field. Especially in Western Europe, deregulation, increasing institutional autonomy, devolution of authority, a shifting balance between state- and market-oriented elements in the steering of higher education systems, and a growing weight of output-related, performance-based factors in steering and sometimes also financing, were the decisive features of that changing relationship. Governments converted their higher education policies from an input-oriented regulation into an output-oriented steering. In general, there was an exchange between deregulation and institutional autonomy on the one hand and quality assurance, accountability and output-control on the other hand.

Furthermore, increasing mobility of students who do not only want to study abroad but also want to have these studies recognised upon return, as well as the heightened opportunities of students to move to places and institutions which they perceive to best respond to their needs, have highlighted the importance of quality assurance and improvement. Finally, the growth of competition from private providers which respond to market needs more flexibly have raised concerns of consumer protection, minimum quality standards and the protection of fundamental academic values. In Eastern Europe, for example, the development of quality assurance and accreditation schemes can to a large extent be attributed to the increasingly complex situation caused by the establishment of numerous private higher education institutions. In the relationship between internationalisation and the quality of higher education three different dimensions can be distinguished:

— the contribution of internationalisation to the improvement of the quality of higher education;

— the quality of internationalisation as such;

— the international dimension of quality assurance systems and mechanisms in higher education.

As van der Wende points out, improving the quality of higher education forms the ultimate goal of many policies and programmes of internationalisation of individual higher education institutions, national governments, and the European Commission. However, that internationalisation should necessarily contribute to quality is by no means guaranteed. Van der Wende lists a number of opportunities and threats connected with internationalisation which can usefully be recalled here:

Opportunities for quality improvement may be found in the broadening and deepening of subject areas by adding international elements (or by joint curriculum development), in staff development, in an enhanced foreign language acquisition and preparation for work in a global economy by study abroad, in the presence of foreign students (the international classroom) and in a greater awareness of the institution of its own quality as compared to international standards and partners. Threats to quality may be related to a loss of control over activities (study and teaching abroad) which take place outside the institution, to teaching new groups of students coming from other countries with unknown learning styles and levels, to teaching and learning in a foreign language (insufficient fluency), and to an excessively external orientation of academics, administrators or managers within the institution."

To van der Wende's list of opportunities, one may add the quality enhancing potential of international cooperation and exposure regarding teaching methodology, new qualification and certification processes, intellectual resource sharing (contributions to the advancement of knowledge), the dissemination of information on a given institution, the improvement of an institution's reputation as well as its management.

Many observers of internationalisation stress that the success of internationalisation increasingly depends on sound quality assurance systems. With mobility and exchange becoming a regular feature of research, teaching and learning, higher education institutions are increasingly forced to let go of their own quality control (to the extent that it existed) and have to trust the host institutions of their outgoing staff or students with respect to the services, infrastructure and expertise offered. If international student and staff mobility continues to increase and if institutions are confronted with more and more demands for credit transfer and recognition of foreign programmes and degrees, their quality assurance mechanisms will have to be extended to also cover the programmes and degrees in foreign partner institutions. Indeed, the growing emphasis on transparency, recognition and credit transfer has further contributed to bringing questions of quality to the foreground.

Already a number of years ago, the then Higher Education Quality Council (HEQC) tried to respond to the growing concerns about the loss of quality control through internationalisation by offering advice and recommendations about quality assurance and standards for institutions of higher education in the UK that have established educational partnerships with other countries. This trend is widely seen to gain momentum. As DeWinter formulates: "In the international 'marriage market', suitors will look in your direction only if you are equipped with a handsome control system. Or, in still other words, the entrance ticket to international educational networks might very well, in the future, become explicitly a sound quality assurance system." Of course, the Maastricht and Amsterdam treaties' articles dealing with higher education emphasise the improvement of the quality of education as the explicit goal of any EU support of higher education cooperation initiatives. This fact makes it all the more remarkable that the emergence of the quality assurance movement in higher education was only influenced to a very limited degree by factors relating to internationalisation and also, until very recently, took very little notice of international aspects of higher education provision.

In many countries, the issues of international competitiveness and international mobility of labour were widely debated and perceived as urgent issues but were nevertheless only marginally (if at all) integrated into debates and development of quality assurance. However, international stimulants have contributed to raising quality awareness and even led to the establishment of quality assurance agencies in some countries.

One example of such stimulants is the Institutional Evaluation Programme of the "European Rectors Conference" (CRE, now officially called the Association of European Universities) which was launched in 1993 in order to help universities improve their quality management processes and assist in developing strategies of change. Over 50 universities have been audited, follow-up visits are being planned.

Another important example were the European pilot projects launched in 1994/95 by the European Commission with the aim of widening experiences of quality evaluation across western Europe. In the framework of these projects, subject evaluations in selected subjects were conducted in 17 countries. These resulted in the creation of several national evaluation agencies in Europe and, eventually, in the founding of a European network of quality assurance agencies which meets regularly to exchange experiences and best practices. In Europe, 11 countries now have quality assurance agencies and more are added each year.

While networking of national agencies has intensified particularly in Europe during the last few years, there also seems to be an increasing interest in such exchanges of experiences and information internationally. The fact that international communication on quality assurance is developing rapidly is evidenced by the emergence of networks, scholarly journals, conferences, and organisations promoting international understanding and mutual exchange of ideas. Recently, to name a prominent example, representatives of quality assurance and accreditation agencies all over the world were hosted by the Council for Higher Education Accreditation (CHEA) in the USA (which is increasingly also pursuing quality assurance interests) with the explicit aim to internationalise quality assurance.

The next steps will focus on exchange of information and good practice and on increasing transparency between the different systems of quality assurance. The same purpose is pursued by the International Network of Quality Assurance Agencies in Higher Education which was formed in the early nineties and holds annual meetings. At the moment, there is still an enormous degree of international variation in quality assurance. Most fundamentally, systems differ in the notions of quality on which they base their operations.

Green distinguishes different concepts of quality: quality as distinctiveness, as conformance to specified standards, as fitness for purpose or effectiveness in achieving institutional goals, and as meeting customers' needs. Also the functions of the quality assurance systems vary greatly: from improving education and giving feed back to higher education staff on teaching, research and curricular design, to allowing for accountability in view of safeguarding the public interest and the efficient use of government funding, to offering public information and market transparency, and finally steering the higher education system through quality indicators in resources and planning. Such different functions of quality assurance naturally entail different emphases, methodologies and operations. Nevertheless, it is to be expected that some degree of convergence will result from the above-mentioned intensification of transnational exchanges of experience, expertise and good practice. Several expert observers see an increasing international convergence in approaches to higher education quality assurance.

Like the internationalisation of quality assurance, the quality of international cooperation itself has also only recently become the subject of focussed networking and cooperative projects. Many obstacles, such as lack of funding, lack of national or institutional commitment and of coherent policies, bureaucratic over-regulation on the part of funding agencies and all kinds of administrative problems (e.g. long application procedures) still hinder the smooth functioning of internationalisation efforts at institutional level, leading to many complaints from students and other participants. Moreover, the actual outcome of individual international cooperation activities is only rarely researched or monitored in detail. In general, widespread systematic evaluation is restricted to analyses of various aspects of student mobility. In spite of the many criticisms of various conditions of international cooperation activities and the generally observed tendency of increased efforts in establishing or expanding quality assurance in higher education, institutional internationalisation activities are as yet only rarely covered by quality assurance procedures since the latter still deal primarily with the "core functions" of education and research. Already in 1994, Smith stated that the assurance of quality should gradually cover the whole spectrum of international dimension activities of a given institution of which he gives an exhaustive and thus useful overview:

— *Academic staff:* teaching assignments and exchanges, sabbaticals abroad, joint curriculum development, intensive courses and summer schools;

— *Students:* arrangements for individual mobility, organised exchanges, study abroad, foreign student reception;

— *Courses and curricula-comparative elements:* international and European elements, area studies, foreign languages (as subjects of study and as medium of delivery), distance learning, use of new technologies;

— *Certification, recognition and assessment:* award of joint/ double degrees, credit transfer arrangements, academic recognition, assessment arrangements;

— *Governance and management:* decision-making structures, international offices, arrangements at faculty/departmental level, staff recruitment, promotion and development, participation in international networks, exchanges of administrative staff, resource management, advisory and information services, evaluation procedures and infrastructure.

Although the need for quality assurance of internationalisation initiatives is increasingly recognised, limited progress has been made towards developing workable systems at national level. Curiously, the above-mentioned EU pilot projects in quality assurance, which had helped the establishment of quality assurance systems in Europe, had also given only very cursory attention to the external relations of universities, as the EAIE remarked. Only in a few countries, codes of practice and specific quality assurance procedures and instruments in the field of international education have been developed. In the UK, as already mentioned, the Higher education Quality Council produced such an instrument which was later developed further by the Quality Assurance Agency. In the Netherlands, institutions' internationalisation policies were reviewed in 1994 by the Inspectorate of higher Education.

The hoge scholen have also developed an instrument for self-evaluation of internationalisation at these higher education institutions which is integrated into the general quality assurance system. In Finland, the Centre for International Mobility (CIMO) developed guidelines for evaluation including institutional self-evaluation of internationalisation, emphasising, like the Dutch, the consistency between the objectives of internationalisation and the institution's wider aims as well as the reflection of these internationalisation objectives in curriculum, organisation, policy development etc. In the US, two quite comprehensive instruments for institutional self-evaluation of internationalisation aiming to estimate the degree of success achieved in internationalisation by a given institution (on a score from 0 to 5) were developed and disseminated a few years ago.

Other countries, many of which have only just begun to establish quality assurance systems, are still far from including the international dimension of higher education in their procedures. Professional organisations, e.g. in business and engineering, have also developed various forms of quality control of education and training in their international networks. Until recently, however, these and other initiatives in developing quality assurance procedures and instruments in international education have been rather dispersed and have remained uncoordinated.

The Internationalisation Quality Review, jointly developed by the OECD and ACA from 1995 onwards, has tried to redress this dispersion. Since 1994, the Programme on Institutional Management in Higher Education (IMHE) of the OECD had had a programme focussing on quality assessment and assurance of institutional-level strategies for the internationalisation of higher education and on the contribution that internationalisation has made to enhancing the quality of higher education.

This concern was now taken up by IQR, through the development (in a first phase) and the refinement (in a second phase) of guidelines for self-assessment and peer review, which assist higher education institutions to assess and enhance the quality of their internationalisation strategies against the background of their own aims and objectives, and thus also to strengthen the contribution that internationalisation makes to the quality of higher education overall. It is to be expected that increasing differentiation among higher education institutions with respect to the quality dimension will result in more discriminating internationalisation policies. Hence, unless the quality issue is fully integrated in internationalisation policies of governments and institutions, the further progress of internalisation is likely to suffer greatly.

The Impact of New Technologies on Internationalisation

Increasingly, new technologies are used to complement and support established cooperation activities, be it mobility or curriculum development. A number of "administrative" examples may serve to illustrate the use of satellites, the Internet, and the World Wide Web in higher education cooperation, such as statistical databases to track students and their progress; Web pages to introduce study abroad options, including detailed information on course work and living situations; the use of e-mail to receive and submit assignments as well as communicate with individual tutors or remain in touch with home students and professors; and online applications to support classroom teaching, providing convenience and saving time. Two broad categories of usage seem to encompass the majority of applications: courses offered over the Internet and the World Wide Web, focusing primarily on students; and research collaboration, focusing on faculty.

The number of courses offered electronically is increasing rapidly. Many of these are prepared and delivered by individual faculty, but often entire units of an institution or indeed entire institutions are being established to offer online alternatives. Especially in the US, the offer of complete degree programmes is available in a growing range of disciplines. One of the best-known providers is the University of Phoenix, an accredited institution in the US offering online undergraduate and graduate courses. In Canada, the Athabasca University is a well-established virtual campus serving thousands of students in Canada and overseas. Traditional universities are also beginning to offer complete degree programmes online. In this new environment, new organisations also emerge, e.g. brokerage organisations, such as the Globewide Network Academy and the Electronic University Network, which help link students with institutions offering courses online, as well as organisations which develop their own courses.

Indeed, with the expansion of the new technologies, a considerable growth of new providers of higher education services can be noted, adding to the choice available to students and to the concerns about minimum quality standards. The upsurge of interest in accreditation in many countries can be linked to these concerns and to the desires of new institutions to receive marketable labels. Indeed, more and more universities of the industrialised world, mostly in Anglo-Saxon countries which tend to adopt a more market-oriented, entrepreneurial approach to the recruitment of students, are not satisfied by the increasing numbers of mobile students coming to them. They combine recruitment of foreign students with extending their educational supply to promising markets in other countries by setting up local campuses under the full authority of the mother institution.

Complete programmes from commencement through graduation are possible in this system, if the local state legally permits the granting of foreign diplomas and degrees on its territory. Here, the process of internationalisation does not only shift from the demand to the supply side but seems to dissolve into a new form of academic imperialism where national offers are simply transferred to another national setting without any guarantee of reflective attention to cultural divergences and intercultural communication.

In some cases, such branch or "off-shore" campuses are indeed seen as an intrusion into the local educational culture and policies of the host country, by offering courses tailored to foreign conditions and needs in a strange environment, mostly in another language and targeted at the more affluent students. A growing number of examples of this form of "internationalisation", which is often misleadingly labelled "transnational education" but should perhaps more fittingly be called neo-imperialism, can be observed, especially but not only in the developing world.

Of course, the most avant-garde development in new forms of higher education provision is the delivery of degree courses by a provider institution situated in one part of the world to other parts of the globe through forms of technologically supported distance education, which is regarded as another form of "transnational education". Information and communication technologies through the Internet and satellite transmission open up avenues of developments in educational delivery modes in which geographical limitations are eliminated. As van Damme observes, "some see the future of global higher education in the emergence of a limited number of global virtual universities, designed by powerful corporations; others think of most current universities providing higher education as well through traditional delivery modes as through virtual modes or, which is highly probable, various intermediate modes." In fact, in most existing forms of distance education there is also face-to-face contact in seminars and workshops in regional support centres in addition to independent learning through electronic delivery of education. In this respect the various "open universities" have done pioneering work, not only in the developed world but also in countries such as Turkey, India, Indonesia, Brazil, etc.

Currently, the eleven most important open universities in the world together enrol about three million students. Also the corporate sector is becoming very active in this field, with multinational corporations such as Microsoft, News Corporation and numerous others. The clearest example of this virtual internationalisation of course is the establishment of real cyber-universities. The International University, "The University of the Web", established in 1993, is the first example of this kind, but others are following. These new institutions offer courses and degree programmes using multiple communication technologies on a global scale. In 1997, the International University has been awarded accreditation in the United States after having obtained GATE-certification.

Another usage of IT for international links, which is more often overlooked or underrated, is the use of IT for the purpose of facilitating collaboration among researchers. We should recall at this point that the World Wide Web itself was actually created in 1989 by Tim Berners-Lee of CERN to facilitate communication between high energy physicists at various distant locations. These collaborations usually occur within a given discipline or thematic area. Secondly and more surprisingly, the organisations which support such collaboration often occur on a regional basis (such as mainly in Europe, or North America, or the Pacific Rim). In order to illustrate the functioning of such IT-based research collaboration, we should briefly describe a single case, the "Upper Atmospheric Research Collaboratory" funded by the National Science Foundation since its beginning in 1992.

This highly developed network fosters distance collaboration between space physicists working together to analyse data from instruments in Greenland. A half-dozen instruments send data on the Internet to scientists at 10 different locations in Michigan, Massachusetts, Maryland, Greenland and Norway. The system allows access to archival and real-time data. The scientist can build multiple "windows" on their individual computers with separate areas for viewing real-time data, archival data and for real-time communication with colleagues using a "chat" function.

The studies of the development of this "collaboratory" have confirmed many of the earlier findings regarding computer-mediated communication: the increased opportunities scientist have to exchange ideas and information with colleagues worldwide and to share scarce expensive resources go hand in hand with the recognition that such long-distance communication requires more structured dialogues, including conscious efforts to establish common understandings about the data.

Listservs are another interesting more informal example of such long distance communication fora among researchers. A listserv is essentially a group of people using e-mail who have joined together to discuss issues of common concern, without any particular goal or task and few constraints on topics which can be raised by members of the list. According to Philson, over 15,000 individual public listservs exist, ranging in membership from a few to over 10,000 individuals, the majority of whom tend to be US participants. Many listservs use a moderator to manage the list and screen messages before broadcasting them to all members of the list. Given the range and exponentially growing scope of all of these IT-based forms of international collaboration it is curious to note that, at the level of policy-making, the link between ICT and distance education on the one hand and internationalisation on the other is often lacking. Moreover, many observers of higher education exchange and politics fear that the challenge from providers of transnational education, distance education, off-shore campuses under the control of another European or overseas institution remains under-estimated, and that neither governments nor higher education institutions are ready to address it as a common issue.

Trends

The State of the art of internationalisation we should highlight five main trends which will be of immediate relevance for the design of EU cooperation with non-member States:

a) The EU's student mobility is well developed but not competitive enough on the international market In 1997, 45,531 Japanese students studied in the US while only 7,708 ended up at European higher education institutions. Although the Japanese example is not representative regarding the size of the gap between Europe and its main competitors,

> we have shown that such data are in principle not singular exceptions but exemplary of a trend which has now firmly established itself and should make any European higher education representative aware of the fact that the Union, more than ever before, has either failed to address mobility obstacles for students from outside of Europe, and failed to sell the advantages of studying in the European Union, or has concentrated too exclusively on its internal market of exchange students.

The imbalance of student mobility flows which increasingly favour the already over-demanded US, but also Canada and Australia over European destinations point to several obstacles with respect to incoming students in Europe: Unlike the US, where regulations were revised in 1990 and now encourage the talented and highly skilled to stay in the US, EU immigration laws still reflect a hostile mistrusting attitude to non-EU students which seem to be regarded as potential immigrants who could take away jobs from locals.

The imminent shortage of highly qualified labour and already dawning shortage of postgraduate students in natural sciences and engineering is not yet taken into account by immigration laws. In this respect, the US, Canada and Australia are a decade ahead in recognising the need for most students from abroad to be able to work part-time, gain professional as well as academic experience during their training and to have some hope of finding a job which responds to their qualifications after their studies. American observers of their own market position mention, for example, the opportunities for US-educated international Ph.D.s on the faculties of American institutions as a competitive advantage. While

European higher education remains far from being widely open to incomers from other countries as far as academic positions are concerned, the pressure from other professional fields is already growing enough to warrant action.

— Professionally designed, concise and widely distributed information in English on European higher education systems as well as on individual higher education institutions and their profiles and strengths is available only to a limited extent. The quality of higher education provision is either not assured systematically or not publicised widely enough wherever it is systematically assured and monitored. Hence, the general inclination of most students from abroad to prefer high-profile destinations and institutions remains unanswered by most European institutions.

— Some of the reputation of the Anglo-Saxon systems of higher education derives from the perception that more attention is paid to the learning process of each student and to the targeted training of his or her competencies. "Learner-centred teaching" and "competence-based learning" have become not only qualitative but also marketable assets of Anglo-Saxon higher education institutions. Continental Europe clearly has something to learn from the attention paid to the learner but also from the more consumer-friendly service culture which developed successfully in the Anglo-Saxon educational (and other) environment. While many services concerning the reception of incoming students have greatly improved in Europe with the quality requirements of such exchange programmes as ERASMUS, much remains to be done, especially with respect to the consumer-friendliness of the "normal" student services and administration.

— The wealth of experience which has been gained in Europe—more than elsewhere—in questions of recognition of study abroad periods and mutual transparency in spite of widely differing systems of education is predominantly used internally but does not seem to be exploited in the wider international cooperation market.

— Beyond mobility, other forms of cooperation gain in importance. In recent years, other forms of cooperation have gained in visibility and emphasis. Teaching staff mobility and joint curriculum development, both activities which presuppose dense communication and exchange between partner institutions, involve academics but also institutional decisions at other levels in order to allow for the adoption of new courses and integration of incoming teaching staff. European institutions of higher education have gained ample experience in this field, more so than institutions elsewhere in the world. Nevertheless, what could be a competitive edge is not exploited as such.

With regard to curriculum development, it would seem all the more surprising that the aggressively expanding market of education products is dominated so strongly by American providers. Such market advantages can only be attributed to the more wide-spread use of ICT, the availability of such course material in English, the will to reach a wider audience and attention paid to doing it justice, and to better marketing of these products. However, it seems that some European countries, such as the UK, which are more advanced in marketing education products, have not been used to the extent possible and desirable, or at any rate not early enough, as an example for others to follow.

— The advance of networking

The rate at which contacts are being established inside and outside Europe is steadily increasing. With the use of ICT, communication and exchange across borders has become even easier so that even multilateral forms of cooperation are transforming from being a communicational challenge into relative normality. European higher education institutions are characterised by a well developed density of such networks of contacts which have often even expanded into inter-institutional networks. Only rarely, however, are such networks used strategically to position the ingredient institutions in a more advantageous manner on the international market, for example by being able to offer pooled expertise in a network of different but complementary specialisation.

d) The quality of cooperation is increasingly regarded as the essential point or stumbling block for sustainable cooperation The international dimension of higher education provision has only recently begun to be subjected to quality assurance. At the same time, quality has become the central focus of European cooperation as more and more contacts accumulate and greater selectivity becomes necessary. With quality enhancement in mind, cooperation activities all over the world are being institutionalised and more frequently integrated into the profile and strategic development of higher education institutions. Helped by national regulations or such cooperation frameworks as SOCRATES, the systematic integration of casuistic cooperation activities into the wider institutional framework, enhancing efficiency as well as the potential for synergies, is taking root in Europe too. It fosters hope that clear strategic targeting and central level attention and prioritisation will push the cause of internationalisation further by greater mobilisation and awareness of the importance of internationalisation for the survival of higher education institutions as well as for better quality assurance and enforceable guidelines of good practice.

Quality management has become the topic of the nineties. Restricted budgets and reduced state interventions have emphasised the role of monitoring and efficient use of public funds. While most individual European countries do not have a tradition of quality assurance agencies overseeing quality enhancement, such agencies have recently been established with the input of already existing systems of quality assurance from other EU member states.

The exchange of information between different agents involved in quality improvement of higher education are increasingly exchanging information and experience. As yet, such progress has not resulted in a qualitatively more transparent European space of higher education, however. Only if the attention paid to issues of quality were to become more visible and effects of quality improvement were to become visible even outside of Europe, would European higher education retrieve its former reputation of offering top-level educational services and research.

e) New technologies and new providers of higher education are challenging the market of international education with new service demands As world-wide communication becomes easier with the help of ICT, the idea of conquering the world market with educational products and services is gaining ground. Business-minded established institutions and profit-based new providers are exploiting these markets aggressively enough to have left more traditional higher education institutions behind. The quality of such offers is by no means better but new demands are being made on the presentation and marketing of any institution which tries to enter the world-wide competition in higher education. The market is generally regarded as a rapidly expanding one with enormous future prospects due to the value attributed to knowledge for economic survival in developed countries. The gold-rush has only started. This time who finds real gold is less a matter of luck but entirely up to the players.

2

Challenges of Globalisation Education

Developing and transition economies face significant new trends in the global environment that affect not only the shape and mode of operation but also the very purpose of tertiary education systems. Among the most critical dimensions of change are the convergent impacts of globalization, the increasing importance of knowledge as a main driver of growth, and the information and communication revolution.

Knowledge accumulation and application have become major factors in economic development and are increasingly at the core of a country's competitive advantage in the global economy. The combination of increased computing power, diminishing prices of hardware and software, improvement of wireless and satellite technologies, and reduced telecommunication costs has all but removed the space and time barriers to information access and exchange. Both opportunities and threats arise from these changes. On the positive side, the role of tertiary education in the construction of knowledge economies and democratic societies is more influential than ever. Indeed, tertiary education is central to the creation of the intellectual capacity on which knowledge production and utilization depend and to the promotion of the lifelong-learning practices necessary to update individual knowledge and skills.

Another favorable development is the emergence of new types of tertiary institutions and new forms of competition, inducing traditional institutions to change their modes of operation and delivery and to take advantage of the opportunities offered by the new information and communication technologies (ICT). But on the negative side, this technological transformation carries the real danger of a growing digital divide between and within nations.

Even as these new opportunities and challenges emerge, most developing and transition countries continue to wrestle with difficulties stemming from inadequate responses to long-standing problems facing their tertiary education systems. Among these unresolved challenges are the need to expand tertiary education coverage in a sustainable way, inequalities of access and outcomes, problems of educational quality and relevance, and rigid governance structures and management practices.

The World Bank has actively supported tertiary education reform efforts in a number of countries. Nevertheless, there is a perception that the Bank has not been fully responsive to the growing demand by clients for tertiary education interventions and that, especially in the poorest countries, lending for the subsector has not matched the importance of tertiary education systems for economic and social development. The Bank is commonly viewed as supporting only basic education; systematically advocating the reallocation of public expenditures from tertiary to basic education; promoting cost recovery and private sector expansion; and discouraging low-income countries from considering any investment in advanced human capital.

Given these perceptions, the rapid changes taking place in the global environment, and the persistence of the traditional problems of tertiary education in developing and transition countries, reexamining the World Bank's policies and experiences in tertiary education has become a matter of urgency. How tertiary education contributes to building up a country's capacity for participation in an increasingly knowledgebased world economy and investigates policy options for tertiary education that have the potential to enhance economic growth and reduce poverty. It examines the following questions: What is the importance of tertiary education for economic and social development? How should developing and transition countries position themselves to take full advantage of the potential contribution of tertiary education? How can the World Bank and other development agencies assist in this process? The ongoing Bank research and analysis on the dynamics of knowledge economies and on science and technology development.

Using this background, it explores how countries can adapt and shape their tertiary education systems to confront successfully the combination of new and old challenges in the context of the rising significance for tertiary education of internal and international market forces. It examines the justification for continuing public support of tertiary education and the appropriate role of the state in support of knowledge-driven economic growth. Finally, it reviews the lessons from recent World Bank experience with support of tertiary education, including ways of minimizing the negative political impact of reforms, and makes recommendations for future Bank involvement. Many of the themes developed in the first World Bank policy on tertiary education, Higher Education: The Lessons of Experience, it emphasizes the following new trends:

— The emerging role of knowledge as a major driver of economic development

— The appearance of new providers of tertiary education in a "borderless education" environment

— The transformation of modes of delivery and organizational patterns in tertiary education as a result of the information and communication revolution

— The rise of market forces in tertiary education and the emergence of a global market for advanced human capital

— The increase in requests from World Bank client countries for financial support for tertiary education reform and development

— The recognition of the need for a balanced and comprehensive view of education as a holistic system that includes not only the human capital contribution of tertiary education but also its critical humanistic and social capital building dimensions and its role as an important global public good.

Briefly, the main messages of this document are as follows:

— Social and economic progress is achieved principally through the advancement and application of knowledge.

— Tertiary education is necessary for the effective creation, dissemination, and application of knowledge and for building technical and professional capacity.

— Developing and transition countries are at risk of being further marginalized in a highly competitive world economy because their tertiary education systems are not adequately prepared to capitalize on the creation and use of knowledge.

— The state has a responsibility to put in place an enabling framework that encourages tertiary education institutions to be more innovative and more responsive to the needs of a globally competitive knowledge economy and to the changing labor market requirements for advanced human capital.

— The World Bank Group can assist its client countries in drawing on international experience and in mobilizing the resources needed to improve the effectiveness and responsiveness of their tertiary education systems.

Tertiary Education Policy in the Context of the World Bank's Development Strategy

As this study shows, support for tertiary education programs contributes to the Bank's overall strategic framework and goals, as outlined below.

Poverty Reduction through Economic Growth

Tertiary education exercises a direct influence on national productivity, which largely determines living standards and a country's ability to compete in the global economy. Tertiary education institutions support knowledge-driven economic growth strategies and poverty reduction by

(a) training a qualified and adaptable labor force, including highlevel scientists, professionals, technicians, teachers in basic and secondary education, and future government, civil service, and business leaders;

(b) generating new knowledge; and

c) building the capacity to access existing stores of global knowledge and to adapt that knowledge to local use.

Tertiary education institutions are unique in their ability to integrate and create synergy among these three dimensions. Sustainable transformation and growth throughout the economy are not possible without the capacity-building contribution of an innovative tertiary education system. This is especially true in low-income countries with weak institutional capacity and limited human capital.

Poverty reduction through redistribution and empowerment

Tertiary education supports the opportunity and empowerment dimensions outlined in World Development 2000/2001. Access to tertiary education can open better employment and income opportunities to underprivileged students, thereby decreasing inequity.

The norms, values, attitudes, ethics, and knowledge that tertiary institutions can impart to students constitute the social capital necessary to construct healthy civil societies and socially cohesive cultures.

Fulfillment of millennium development goals

It is doubtful that any developing country could make significant progress toward achieving the United Nations Millennium Develoment Goals (MDGs) for education-universal enrollment in primary education and elimination of gender disparities in primary and secondary education-without a strong tertiary education system. Tertiary education supports the rest of the education system through the training of teachers and school principals, the involvement of specialists from tertiary education institutions in curriculum design and educational research, and the establishment of admission criteria that influence the content and methods of teaching and learning at the secondary level. A similar argument applies to the contribution of postsecondary medical education, especially the training of medical doctors, epidemiologists, public health specialists, and hospital managers, to meeting the basic health MDGs.

The state and tertiary education

Research on the dynamics of knowledge-driven development has identified the converging roles of four contributing factors: a country's macroeconomic incentive and institutional regime, its ICT infrastructure, its national innovation system, and the quality of its human resources. Of these, the contribution of tertiary education is vital with respect to the national innovation system and the development of human resources. In this context, continued government support of tertiary education is justified by three important considerations: the existence of externalities from tertiary education, equity issues, and the supportive role of tertiary education in the education system as a whole.

Externalities

Investments in tertiary education generate major external benefits that are crucial for knowledge-driven economic and social development. Private investment in tertiary education can be suboptimal because individuals do not capture all the benefits of education. Afew examples will illustrate how education yields benefits to society as a whole. Technological innovations and the diffusion of scientific and technical innovations lead to higher productivity, and most of these innovations are the products of basic and applied research undertaken in universities. Progress in the agriculture, health, and environment sectors, in particular, is heavily dependent on the application of such innovations.

Higher skill levels in the labor force-an outcome of increased educational levels-and the qualitative improvements that permit workers to use new technology also boost productivity. Tertiary education facilitates nation building by promoting greater social cohesion, trust in social institutions, democratic participation and open debate, and appreciation of diversity in gender, ethnicity, religion, and social class. Furthermore, pluralistic and democratic societies depend on research and analysis that are fostered through social sciences and humanities programs. Improved health behaviors and outcomes also yield strong social benefits, and higher education is indispensable for training the needed health care professionals.

Equity

Imperfections in capital markets limit the ability of individuals to borrow sufficiently for tertiary education, thereby hindering the participation of meritorious but economically disadvantaged groups. Although more than 60 countries have student loan programs, access to affordable loans frequently remains restricted to a minority of students. Moreover, these loans are not necessarily available to the students with limited resources who most need financial aid. Very few countries have national programs reaching more than 10 percent of the student population, and these exceptions are rich countries such as Australia, Canada, Sweden, the United Kingdom, and the United States. In addition, where they do exist, student loans are not always available for the whole range of academic programs and disciplines.

Support for other levels of the education system

Tertiary education plays a key role in supporting basic and secondary education, thereby buttressing the economic externalities produced by these lower levels. Improved tertiary education is necessary for sustainable progress in basic education. The supply of qualified teachers and school leaders, capacity for curriculum design, research on teaching and learning, economic analysis and management-these and many more components of basic education reform are hampered by weak tertiary education systems.

A comprehensive approach to the development of the education sector is required, along with a balanced distribution of budgetary resources to ensure that countries invest appropriately in tertiary education, with attention to their progress toward the Millennium Development Goals. When looking at the public benefits of tertiary education, it is important to note the existence of joint-product effects linked to the complementarity between tertiary education and the lower levels of education, as described above, and between undergraduate and postgraduate education.

While many undergraduate and professional education programs can be offered in separate institutions (business and law are examples), high-cost activities such as basic research and various types of specialized graduate training are more efficiently organized in combination with undergraduate training. Cross-subsidization across educational disciplines, programs, and levels leads to public-good effects that are valuable but are difficult to quantify. In addition, there are economies of scale that justify public support of expensive programs such as basic sciences that are almost natural monopolies.

Determining appropriate investment levels

Notwithstanding the methodological difficulties involved in measuring externalities, the existence of these important public benefits indicates that the costs of insufficient investment in tertiary education can be very high. These costs can include reduced ability of a country to compete effectively in global and regional economies; a widening of economic and social disparities; declines in the quality of life, in health status, and in life expectancy; an increase in unavoidable public expenditures on social welfare programs; and a deterioration of social cohesion. Sustainable transformation and growth throughout the economy cannot be achieved without an innovative tertiary education system to help build the absorptive capacity that is required if private sector investment and donor resources are to have a lasting productive impact.

At the same time, the development of a holistic education system calls for a comprehensive approach to resource allocation. Certain guidelines can be applied to ensure a balanced distribution of budgetary resources and an appropriate sequencing of investment across the three education subsectors in relation to a country's level of education development, pattern of economic growth, and fiscal situation. Based on the experience of industrial countries that have emphasized the role of education in supporting economic growth and social cohesion, it would seem that an appropriate range for the overall level of investment in education as a share of gross domestic product (GDP) would be between 4 and 6 percent. In this context, expenditures on tertiary education would generally represent between 15 and 20 percent of all expenditures on public education. Developing countries that devote more than 20 percent of their education budget to tertiary education, especially those that have not attained universal primary education coverage, are likely to have a distorted allocation that favors an elitist university system and does not adequately support basic and secondary education. Similarly, countries that spend more than 20 percent of their tertiary education budget on noneducational expenditures such as student subsidies are likely to be underinvesting in materials, equipment, library resources, and other inputs that are crucial for quality learning.

The evolving role of the state

As their direct involvement in the funding and provision of tertiary education diminishes, governments rely less on the traditional state control model to make reforms happen. Instead they promote change by guiding and encouraging tertiary education institutions through a coherent policy framework, an enabling regulatory environment, and appropriate financial incentives.

1. Countries and tertiary education institutions willing to take advantage of the new opportunities presented by the knowledge economy and the ICT revolution must be proactive in fostering innovations and launching meaningful reforms in a coherent policy framework. Although there is no blueprint that is valid for all countries, a common prerequisite seems to be a clear vision for the long-term development of a comprehensive, diversified, and well-articulated tertiary education system. Student mobility can be encouraged by developing open systems that offer recognition of relevant prior experience, degree equivalencies, credit transfer, tuition exchange schemes, access to national scholarships and student loans, and a comprehensive qualifications and lifelong-learning framework.

2. The regulatory environment should be one that encourages rather than stifles innovations in public institutions and initiatives by the private sector to

expand access to good-quality tertiary education. Rules for the establishment of new institutions, including private and virtual ones, should be restricted to outlining minimum quality requirements and should not constitute barriers to entry. Other regulatory considerations should be the development of quality assurance mechanisms (evaluation, accreditation, national examinations, rankings, and publication of information), financial controls to which public institutions are required to conform, and intellectual property rights legislation.

3. Although public funding remains the main source of support for tertiary education in most countries, it is being channeled in new ways and is being increasingly supplemented by nonpublic resources. Both of these changes bring market forces to bear in ways heretofore uncommon in the financing of public institutions. New financing strategies have been put in place in the public sector to generate revenue from institutional assets, to mobilize additional resources from students and their families, and to encourage donations from thirdparty contributors. Many governments have also encouraged the creation of private institutions as an effective approach for easing pressures on the public purse and satisfying pent-up demand.

World Bank Support for Tertiary Education

In the 1970s and 1980s much of the support provided by World Bank tertiary education projects was piecemeal, with a narrow focus on the establishment of new programs or on discrete quality improvement measures for existing teaching and research activities. These projects sometimes created well-equipped academic oases-which tended to become unsustainable over time. The Bank was rarely able to offer the type of longterm comprehensive support for tertiary education that is required for successful reform and effective institution building.

An internal review of implementation experience with tertiary education projects undertaken in 1992 and an assessment of recent and ongoing interventions in this subsector have offered critical insights into more productive ways of supporting tertiary education reforms and innovations. Three vital lessons emerge from past and current tertiary education projects, as outlined below.

Comprehensive reforms can be more effective than piecemeal ones. Interventions integrated into a broad reform program based on a global change strategy are more likely to bear fruit than isolated efforts. Financing reforms, especially the introduction of tuition fees and the expansion of private tertiary education, are difficult to implement successfully without equity measures to help disadvantaged students gain access to and afford tertiary education. They also require significant devolution of government control in matters affecting institutional costs, as well as incentives for institutions to engage in cost-saving and income-generating activities. The preference for comprehensiveness does not mean that all aspects of a reform should be packed into a single operation. Sequencing provides the tools for responding to and adjusting to evolving challenges. Long-term involvement through a series of complementary operations, as occurred in China, Indonesia, the Republic of Korea, and Tunisia, has proved essential for ensuring structural change that is sustainable.

Attention to the political-economy aspects of reform is vital. Until the beginning of the 1990s, little attention was paid to the political economy of tertiary education reforms, on the assumption that a technically sound reform program and agreement with top government officials were all that was needed for change to succeed. But when it came to actual implementation, political reality often proved stronger than the technocratic vision. In many countries various interest groups have resisted proposed reform programs. Launching and implementing tertiary education reforms has been more successful when decisionmakers have managed to build a consensus among the various constituents of the tertiary education community.

Reliance on positive incentives to promote change can be pivotal. The extent to which projects rely on positive incentives rather than mandatory edicts to stimulate change has a great influence on outcomes, as institutions and actors tend to respond more readily to constructive stimuli. The World Bank has had positive experience with such policy instruments as competitive funds, accreditation mechanisms, and management information systems. Well designed competitive funds and incentives encourage better performance by tertiary education institutions and can be powerful vehicles for transformation and innovation, as demonstrated by the positive results of projects in Argentina, Chile, the Arab Republic of Egypt, Guinea, and Indonesia.

Directions for future Bank support

Investment in tertiary education is an important pillar of development strategies that emphasize the construction of democratic, knowledgebased economies and societies. The World Bank can play a central role by facilitating policy dialogue and knowledge sharing, supporting reforms through program and project lending, and promoting an enabling framework for the production of the global public goods crucial to the development of tertiary education.

Facilitating policy dialogue and knowledge sharing

Reform proposals that are likely to affect established practices and vested interests are always met with fierce resistance and opposition from those groups most affected by the intended redistribution of power and wealth. Under the right circumstances, the Bank may play a catalytic role by encouraging and facilitating the policy dialogue on tertiary education reforms. This can often be accomplished through preemptive information sharing and analytical work in support of national dialogue and goal-setting efforts, as well as through project preparation activities aimed at building stakeholder consensus during the project concept and appraisal phases.

The Bank can bring to the same table stakeholders who would not normally converse and work together. It can also share information on a great variety of national and institutional experiences that can nourish the debate in any country and that offer objective reference points for analysis of the local situation and assessment of the range and content of policy options worth considering. This type of dialogue can assist in the formulation of a long-term vision for the country's tertiary education system as a whole and in the preparation of strategic plans at the level of individual institutions. The World

Bank's comparative advantage in relation to other donor agencies in supporting policy dialogue in client countries stems from two related factors.

— The Bank has access to worldwide experiences that can be shared with interested counterparts and stakeholders.

— It can tie reform of tertiary education to economywide reform. The comprehensive nature of the Bank's work allows it to adopt a systemwide approach linking sectoral issues to the overall development framework and public finance context of any country, rather than focus on isolated interventions in support of specific institutions.

In supporting the actual implementation of tertiary education reforms, the World Bank gives priority to programs and projects that can bring about positive developments and innovations by:

— Increasing institutional diversification (growth of nonuniversity and private institutions) to expand coverage on a financially viable basis and establish a lifelong-learning framework with multiple points of entry and multiple pathways

— Strengthening science and technology research and development capacity in selected areas linked to a country's priorities for the development of comparative advantages

— Improving the relevance and quality of tertiary education

— Promoting greater equity mechanisms (scholarships and student loans) intended to create and expand access and opportunities for disadvantaged students

— Establishing sustainable financing systems to encourage responsiveness and flexibility

— Strengthening management capacities, through such measures as introduction of management information systems, to promote improved accountability, administration, and governance and more efficient utilization of existing resources

— Enhancing and expanding information technology and communications capacity to reduce the digital divide (complementing existing global initiatives by the World Bank such as the Global Development Learning Network, the African Virtual University, the Global Development Network, and World Links).

The lessons of recent experience show that Bank support to client countries should be:

— Appropriate to a country's specific circumstances

— Predicated on strategic planning at national and institutional levels

— Focused on promoting autonomy and accountability

— Geared toward enhancing institutional capacity and facilitating the cross-fertilization of relevant regional experiences

— Sequenced, with a time horizon consistent with the long-term nature of capacity enhancement efforts

— Sensitive to local political considerations affecting tertiary education reform.

The relative emphasis and mix of interventions appropriate for any given country are linked to its specific political and economic circumstances both at the macroeconomic level and in tertiary education. Income level, country size, and political stability are all important factors. In setting priorities for the appropriate mix of lending and nonlending services in a given country, the Bank will be guided by the following criteria:

(a) the need to change (the gravity of the issues and the urgency of reform) and

(b) willingness to reform, as reflected in the government's commitment to implementing meaningful change and its ability to mobilize major stakeholders in support of the reform agenda.

In countries where the need for reform is acute, the choice of lending instrument should be guided by the following considerations:

— Adaptable program loans (APLs) are preferred in countries with a strategic framework and expectations of political stability, as they facilitate a systemwide, holistic, long-term approach. When necessary, the first phase of the APLcould focus on consolidating the strategic framework for reform and on building consensus among all stakeholders.

— Budget support can be extended in the context of programs for the education sector as a whole in countries where the tertiary education reform agenda is a high priority and where there is a clear commitment from all stakeholders to support the proposed reforms.

— Technical assistance loans (TALs) or learning and innovation loans (LILs) are appropriate where there is government interest in initiating change in the tertiary education sector but the conditions for implementing a reform are not fully met (that is, when there is high need but low political will).

Countries should use TALs to help formulate a comprehensive reform strategy and build a national consensus around it. LILs should be used to pilot innovations before they are replicated on a larger scale.

— International Finance Corporation (IFC) loans and guarantees in support of individual private institutions can be extended to complement International Bank for Reconstruction and Development (IBRD) loans in countries that have established a positive regulatory and incentives framework to promote private tertiary education. IBRD lending that involves private tertiary education would focus on systemwide interventions for quality improvement and accreditation (using competitive funding) or for the establishment of student loan schemes for the entire private sector.

Most of the options outlined above are directly relevant to middleincome countries. Important distinctions are warranted, however, for three groups of World Bank clients: transition countries, low-income countries, and small states. Such countries operate under special conditions that require a different focus and set of priorities.

— The leading options for improving tertiary education in the transition countries of Eastern Europe and Central Asia include introducing more flexible and less specialized curricula, promoting shorter programs and courses, creating a more adaptable regulatory framework, and establishing systems of public funding that encourage institutions to respond to market demands for quality and diversity. Other important options include improving access through the provision of financial aid to students, requiring external participation in governance, and professionalizing university administration. Public investments are needed to build capacity for academic and management innovation, to expand the breadth of course offerings at individual institutions, and to create new programs in response to evolving demand-driven areas of learning.

Directions for tertiary education development for low-income countries would have three priorities:

(a) building capacity for managing and improving the basic and secondary education system, including capacity for training and retraining teachers and principals;

(b) expanding the production of qualified professionals and technicians through a cost-effective combination of public and private nonuniversity institutions; and

(c) making targeted investments in fields of advanced training and research in chosen areas of comparative advantage.

In countries that rely on poverty reduction strategy credits, the focus should be on resource rationalization measures to ensure balanced development of the entire education sector; on an effective contribution by tertiary education to the country's Education for All program, especially through the teacher training institutions; and on the capacity-building role of tertiary education to promote the achievement of the other MDGs (agriculture, health, environment) and facilitate economic diversification efforts.

— In addressing the tertiary education needs of small states, the top priorities are

(a) subregional partnerships with neighboring small states to establish a networked university;

(b) strategically focused tertiary education institutions that address a very limited proportion of the nation's critical human skill requirements;

(c) negotiated franchise partnerships between the national government and external providers of tertiary education; and

(d) government-negotiated provision of distance education by a recognized international provider.

Enabling framework for global public goods

Globalization and the growth of borderless education raise important issues that affect tertiary education in all countries but are often beyond the control of any one national government. Among these challenges are new forms of human capital flight ("brain drain") that result in a loss of local capacity in fields critical to development; the absence of a proper international accreditation and qualifications framework; the absence of accepted legislation regarding foreign tertiary education providers; the lack of clear intellectual property regulations governing distance education programs; and barriers to access to information and communication technologies, including the Internet. The World Bank is uniquely positioned to work with its partners in the international community to promote an enabling framework for the global public goods that are crucial for the future of tertiary education.

Brain drain issues. The following measures could be envisaged for dealing with brain drain:

(a) increased reliance on joint degrees;

(b) inclusion in donor-funded scholarships of allocations for purchasing the minimum equipment and materials needed by returning scholars and for travel to update knowledge;

(c) a preference for sending grantees to top-quality training institutions in other developing countries that possess an oversupply of skilled labor, such as India; and

(d) creation of a favorable local work environment for national researchers and specialists.

International quality assurance framework: In addition to the support provided through accreditation components in specific country projects, the World Bank will contribute toward the goal of establishing an international qualifications framework through consultations with donors and specialized professional associations, as well as through the Development Grant Facility. Two sets of complementary initiatives will be considered:

(a) technical and financial assistance to groups of small countries that wish to set up a regional quality assurance system in lieu of separate national ones and

(b) support for global quality assurance initiatives on a thematic basis.

Trade barriers: The World Bank will work at both international and national levels to help define rules of conduct and appropriate safeguards designed to protect students from low quality offerings and fraudulent providers, without allowing these mechanisms to constitute rigid entry barriers. Governments, licensing bodies, and tertiary education institutions could apply the following criteria to evaluate foreign providers that are not yet accredited by an internationally recognized agency:

(a) minimum infrastructure, facilities, and staffing requirements;

(b) appropriate, transparent, and accurate information on the policies, mission statements, study programs, and feedback mechanisms of foreign providers, including the channels for complaints and appeals;

(c) capacity-building partnerships between foreign providers and local institutions; and

(d) comparable academic quality and standards, including the full recognition in the home country of the degrees and qualifi- cations delivered by foreign providers in a developing country.

Intellectual property rights. The World Bank will play a brokering role to help create and nurture dissemination partnerships among publishing companies, universities in advanced nations, and tertiary education institutions in developing countries. This could be done along the lines of the decision by the Massachusetts Institute of Technology to offer all its courses free of charge on the Web, or the recently announced agreement among six leading publishers of medical journals to give free access to their journals to more than 600 institutions in the 60 poorest countries.

Bridging the digital gap: As part of its strategic commitment to global public goods, the World Bank will contribute to decreasing the digital divide between industrial and developing countries by supporting investments in ICT infrastructure for tertiary education within countries or even in mul:iple countries, as is happening under the Millennium Science Initiative. In conclusion, the Bank aspires to apply its extensive knowledge base and financial resources toward increased efforts in the tertiary education sector. Strengthening the capacity of tertiary education institutions to respond flexibly to the new demands of knowledge societies will increase their contribution to poverty reduction through the long-term economic effects and the associated welfare benefits that come from sustained growth.

Globalisation Apartheid—The Role of Higher Education in Development

Globalisation as a concept in this chapter is not used from an ideological point of view but rather as an economic process that tries to integrate world economies. Globalisation - particularly the removal of barriers to free trade, and the integration of national economies has potential as a force for reducing poverty levels in the world. The problems in reaching those goals (poverty reduction) are mainly due to policies adopted, the management of those processes, the politics in decision-making, and lack of representation from those whose lives are directly affected by globalisation. Views from the South that could inform those policies are often ignored by international development agencies. Academic debates on these issues try to incorporate other views but the outcomes of those debates seldom have direct impact on development policies. Recently at the World Summit on Sustainable Development (WSSD) President Mbeki in addressing a crowd of protesters mentioned that the greatest enemy to development is global apartheid.

Representatives at the WSSD objected to because of the concept apartheid because of its association with South Africa's former government's deliberate move to discriminate against people of different racial backgrounds. The implications are that there is no deliberate intention to treat countries differently in the new economic process. The issue is debatable because there is evidence of global apartheid around - the gap between the rich and the poor has widened more in the last decades as poverty levels rose.

There is evidence of the devastation of globalisation on developing countries as the poverty gap has increased despite the fact that globalisation was meant to benefit all members of the global community. To date it is estimated that about 40 percent of families in the world survive on less than one dollar per day. This is in contrast to the subsidies given to farmers in countries like the US where the subsidy is about $1.00 per day per animal. The G8 Summit of June 2002 refused to address the issue of subsidies provided for in the United States Farm Bill that perpetuates over-production and export dumping that undermine agriculture in Africa.

The new farm Bill announced around April 2002 is aimed at increasing U.S farm subsidies by $35 billion and that translates to more than $20000 to each farme. The negative impact of globalisation has been felt more by those in developing countries. For example, Africa has had a 4% decline in GDP - a decline in per capita income that has resulted in a drop of living standards. This has happened within a context where the world income has increased annually by 2.5%.

Apartheid was defined as an empowering strategy through the separation of races, the unequal distribution of resources and privileges, and preservation of cultures. Policies were decided upon by the dominant minority with power who tried to justify the need for people of different races to develop separately, whilst remaining connected and being dependent on each other. The global economy operates with comparable strategies and policies to those that were adopted by the repressive, former government of South Africa.

Change to power sharing in South Africa was brought about through strategies that included the mobilization of masses for mass protests. International activists have adopted similar strategies as evident through scenes of conflict at World Trade Organization meetings, United Nations Conferences, World Bank and IMF meetings in DC. World politics are intertwined with policies for development and impact negatively on development strategies. Speakers at the WSSD complained about how the Summit agenda was dominated by EU and US views that imposed their own perceptions and definition of humanity.

At the end the US stood alone due to its hard-side, refusing to set targets on the eradication of poverty and undoing environmental damage as part of the strategy for sustainable development. Globalisation is characterized by increased connectedness as well as major inequities between countries and within countries. The digital divide between the North and South often presented in globalisation debates is real but also problematic in the sense that the division cannot only be explained in terms of the division between the North and South, because there are cities in the North that are worse or similar to some cities in the South. There is poverty and illiteracy in the North and instances where people live under worse conditions than those in the South. There are also pockets of technological advancements in both the North and the South that shifts the parameters to the "haves" and "have nots" rather than just the North and the South.

Overall globalisation apartheid has had a devastating effect on developing countries. There have been acknowledgements from the World Bank and the British Department for International Development that the benefits of globalisation are not being passed on to Sub-Saharan Africa and instead globalisation has exacerbated many of Africa's problems. Africa and as a result the percentage of trade has dropped in the last two decades. There are warnings and signals of the possibility that developing countries are at risk of being excluded from the dynamics of the world economy. The situation there is need to radically rethink policies imposed on developing countries in areas such as trade agreements. He further argues that for globalisation to benefit all, there is need to share growth in a more equitable way.

Higher Education and Development

The role of education in development is slowly becoming unclear and more rhetorical in debates on globalisation and development. So far lack of economic development mainly in countries of the South has been, inter alia, been blamed on low participation rates in higher education. In response some of the countries in East Asia adopted a strategy of designing their education systems to help close the knowledge and technology gap between them and the North. Their economies improved until the recent financial crisis that impacted negatively on those countries. There is need to raise the issue of the role of higher education in development in the context of regions such as Africa where nearly half of Sub-Saharan Africa's 600 million people live on less than $1.00 a day, more than a third of children are malnourished, people are dying of AIDS with minimal improvements in education and health. There is data that correlates levels of development to levels of participation in education.

There are convincing arguments to increase participation rates in education both as a human right and a strategy for development. These arguments seem to be presented in different forums discussing strategies for development and remain unconnected to debates by intellectuals in the education field. The role of higher education on the development agenda such as those of the United Nations Millennium Development Goals or the WSSD is not clear and of concern. The United Nations, on Sustainable development warned of education being in the danger of becoming a forgotten priority of the Rio meeting on sustainable development.

The 1992 Rio meeting had put education on the agenda but failed to specify the role of higher education. At the 2002 Johannesburg higher education stakeholders participated through a Consortium referred to as "The Linked Consortia for Environmental and Development - Industry and Urban Areas" as a way of ensuring that higher education becomes part of the development agenda. An interesting observation is that countries from the North were not represented on the consortium except Denmark. Another example of lack of clarity on the role of higher education in development is the notable absence of higher education participation in the development of Africa's renewal strategy " The New

Partnership for Africa's Development" (NEPAD). The presentation of this strategy to leaders of powerful nations in Canada recently by a delegation of three African heads of State led by Thabo Mbeki (President of South Africa) did not receive the anticipated response indicating high commitment to assist Africa by supporting the development strategy for Africa. Five heads of state presented the plan to the United Nations Assembly 2002.

There was criticism of the plan, particularly its failure to consult widely within the continent but it received a lot of support. NEPAD represents a shift in strategy by African governments from relying on aid for development to demanding a change in trading relationships between the North and South because trade has more potential for development than aid. Planned NEPAD projects require huge amounts of money to implement and partnership with the North is sought in that regard. In the globalizing economy higher education has featured on the WTO agenda not for its contribution to development but more as a service to trade in or a commodity for boosting income for countries that have the ability to trade in this area and export their higher education programs.

Higher education has become a multi-billion dollar market as the quantity of education is increasing rapidly and double every five years. The export of higher education service has contributed significantly to the economy of the US. In 1999 it is estimated that the US, being the largest provider of education services, earned $8,5 billion of the $30 billion market, from this trade alone. The share for Asia is estimated at $10 billion. Higher education has in the past contributed to development by providing national economies with the necessary human resources but criticized for not dealing directly with poverty reduction issues. The recent World Bank, still in draft from, on higher education presents an argument for the indirect role that higher education can play in development and in poverty reduction as part of the World Bank's development strategy.

There are three key arguments are presented. The first argument is that higher education can contribute to economic growth by supplying the necessary human resources for a knowledge driven economy, by generating knowledge, and by promoting access and use of knowledge. The second argument is that higher education has the potential of increasing access to education and in turn increasing the employability of those who have the skills for a knowledge driven economy. The third argument is that higher education could play a role in supporting basic and secondary education by supplying those sub-sectors with trained personnel and contributing to the development of the curriculum.

There is need to rethink the role of higher education in national development as national economies are slowly been replaced by a global economy and national higher education is being slowly replaced by global systems of higher education. Higher education role has shifted more to supporting an economy that is knowledge intensive at a global level. The relevance of higher education systems at local level needs to be rethought in the framework of their relevance in the global context, hence the question as to whether they are still relevant to development at a local level. The issue is of concern as the public good of systems of higher education operating at a global level is debatable. There is a renewal of higher education systems of education in countries of the South and a renewed interest by the donor agencies operating in Africa to support higher education. At national levels new reform policies are being developed and at institutional levels new leadership has embarked on the processes to revive their institutions and write new strategic development plans. International agencies such as the World Bank have also revised their policies towards supporting higher education and have come to accept the view that there is need for investment at all levels of education as a strategy for promoting development. Changes taking place have put a lot of emphasis on the need for accountability to society beyond financial accountability, demand for intellectual leadership, and partnership that could contribute to development.

Promoting Cooperation within a Competitive Environment

> "The more we become integrated in the world economy, the more we are under pressure to increase our competitiveness, the more we need to have education of higher quality than we have today."

One of the key features of globalization is increased competition. Competition has become a driving force for innovation and entrepreneurship. Competition in higher education has increased and has become unfair. Countries of the North with their competitive advantage compete with countries from the South for best students, faculty, administrators, and researchers. As a result the intellectual resource from the South are been drained in the process. Sources of high-level skilled labor for the thriving global economy have been mainly the developing countries and Russia during its transition to a capitalist economy. Articles in "The Chronicle of Higher Education", on the concerns over the brain drain in developing countries including Africa. It is estimated that Africa has lost 100,000 people with specialized skill to the West.

The loss is estimated at about 23,000 qualified academic professionals each year for Africa. Most academics are Egypt, Ghana, Kenya, Nigeria, and South Africa. Russia, a loss of 30,000 researchers. Brain drain to be the greatest obstacles to development. Countries from the South are at risk of being further marginalized if their higher education institutions fail to participate in the knowledge production networks and activities that would make them relevant and more responsive to the needs of a new economy.

A concern has been raised by academics from the South about lack of collegiality and concern amongst academics from the South and those from the North within a competitive environment. Competition has resulted in student losses to private for profit higher education, loss of jobs, and in some cases the threat of closure of institutions. Competition in academia has continued to perpetuate the negative effect of globalization such as increasing inequality both between academics within institutions and between academics in different institutions and countries. Trade piracy within a globalizing context and in general has become a problem too for many countries and costs countries a lot in losses despite the adoption of tough laws by organizations such as the World Trade Organization. International companies and institutions are flooding developing countries with cheap products. In higher education trade, inferior programs that are costly are offered to students in countries of the South especially in countries where there are no quality control mechanisms in place.

Even in situations where there are some control measures in place there are institutions that manage to slip through control measures and students are ripped off. The situation has become problematic and some countries find it difficult to protect what they value in education in the same way that countries in the North do. South Africa responded by declaring a moratorium on new partnerships in distance education during a period of transformation whilst putting in place quality control mechanisms.

To promote co-operation within a competitive environment there is need to consider current institutional responses to global changes and perceived threat posed by increased competition. Universities in the South have responded differently to the challenges they face under globalisation. Moja and Cloete categorized the responses based on their study of the higher education landscape in South Africa as follows:

a) *The need to compete and increase the market share:* This has happened in institutions where institutions have reluctantly embraced the changes and have responded by adopting market strategies for change. Attention is paid to strategic planning recognizing and distinguishing between the core business and non-core business resulting in the outsourcing of non-core business activities. Students are treated as clients, budgeting is organized into cost centers, and management emphasize efficiency in all operations at an institution. New funding mechanisms are sought out including a push for contract research in knowledge production.

b) *The need to focus on local changes and ignore global changes:* This has happened in institutions that have been focusing more on internal politics driven by recent political changes in South Africa. These institutions have been restructuring their governance structures to be in line with legislative requirements. Due to conflicts between stakeholders and leadership and transformation demands on leadership, and financial problems, those institutions have as not yet even started responding to global changes taking place.

c) *The need to fight new cultural imperialists:* This has happened in institutions where there is perceived threat of a take over by foreign providers of higher education. Some institutions have asked government to protect them from "foreign invaders" and government responded by releasing a moratorium on new distance education programs as already mentioned. Other institutions opted to fight by competing in the global world and a South African institution, for example, was granted a contract against British institutions to offer health distance education programs in Turkey and Israel. Other strategies for fighting have been to form partnerships with the private sector in delivering educational programs to masses of students tapping new sources and increasing institutional budgets.

National responses to globalization vary from innovations driven by the need for survival to increased competition and becoming more entrepreneurial.

Institutions mainly in Europe have opted to become more entrepreneurial 13 and the newly appointed president at New York University has been pushing an agenda for an enterprise university. The newly formed European Consortia of Innovative Universities (ECIU) is another example and the emerging literature on entrepreneur universities. There are countries that have embraced the changes and some developing countries have even signed for participation in the General Agreement on Trade in Service (GATS). Hong Kong for example has opted to embrace the changes taking place and capitalize on the opportunities offered to increase access to higher education. Countries that have been unable to increase participation rates due to financial constraints have also opted for opening up their countries for global foreign providers as a cheaper option than investing in the needed infrastructure.

The issue to be raised is whether it is possible to cooperate within a competitive environment. The private sector offers some lessons on strategic partnership when necessary in order to become more competitive. In higher education opportunities for cooperation are created by the emergence of multiple, networked, global knowledge production sites as higher education increasingly looses the monopoly for knowledge production. Two challenges arise for universities in the South. The first is a challenge of becoming part of the networks and the second is the challenge of producing knowledge or using knowledge for development purposes. With the latter, institutions are finding themselves paying more attention to meeting the need for increasing access at the expense of research. Faculty teaching loads have been increasing - leaving little room for research, as survival has become more dependent on fee paying students.

Universities from the North have generally responded to globalization by establishing partnerships with other knowledge producers and participation in innovation hubs. Universities in the South need to be part of the new arrangements being forged in the North in knowledge production, dissemination and reconfiguration for production. Emerging social relations so far largely exclude universities from the South. There is need to include universities of the South in the new trans-institutional arrangements for the development of knowledge production sites and multiple agencies involved in the production and dissemination of knowledge. If there is no cooperation in involving universities from the South in such arrangements there is a danger that the gap between the poor and the rich nations will not be widened.

Universities from the South have already been indirectly affected by the new market operations in the new information production and dissemination strategies. The universities from the North have recruited the best students, faculty, and researchers from their counterparts in the South. Some institutions, for example, in South Africa have also lost their best senior administrators to the countries in the North and their best students to the institutions that had the best facilities provided by the former discriminatory government. There is need to cooperate in capacity building for those institutions that in some cases have paid little or no attention to knowledge production due to financial constraints. Partnership between universities could contribute to capacity building in knowledge production and use of knowledge, in delivering and disseminating knowledge to masses of students, in contributing to the development of human resources with high-level skills that in turn could contribute to development. In considering cooperative and partnership arrangements, universities in the North need to address some of the concerns raised by universities in the South and their responses to global changes and increased competition.

— There is general concern that with the changes taking place globally, countries of the South are at risk of having their local concerns overlooked or ignored. The response in some instances has been to make a shift from basic research to applied research. For example, knowledge production trends in South Africa indicate a shift to addressing more of the national concerns. There is evidence that overall knowledge production figures have dropped but there is more contract research conducted at institutions that is directed at strategic (socio-economic and industry) goals.

— There is concern over lack of sensitivity to the cultural bias of exported education and the negative impact competition could have on institutions as it erodes the best human resources resulting in the decay or closure of closure of institutions.

— There is concern over partnerships that might perpetuate inequalities amongst institutions and amongst students within the same institution. For example, a private sector and public sector partnerships that aimed at delivering education to the masses could result in the short changing of poor students receiving their education through those arrangements. The often-cited success story of innovations at Makerere University has been criticized in some quarters for creating inequalities amongst students taking the same courses. The partnership between Tufts University and Makerere University in delivering a political science course using technology allows some and not the whole class to participate in the interactions. The emerging inequalities have become common in countries with free higher education systems but with provision for the intake of fee-paying students to supplement institutional income.

Universities in the South need to take the initiative in strengthening themselves to be able to respond to the needs of a new global economy. An example of a model geared toward enabling universities to take the initiative in their revival is that presented by the Foundation Partnership for "Strengthening African Universities". The partnership has decided to provide support to institutions in Africa that are responding to new challenges posed by globalisation and the need to respond to changing societal needs.

The support is provided in the form of grants to institutions to develop and implement strategic plans, support for research on change in African universities, support to university leadership to participate in global networks and professional associations, and promoting debates on change and the role of universities for development. The foundations provide support over an extended period whilst institutions work on mechanisms for sustainability. Private and public sector cooperation could contribute to development. Higher education systems of some developing countries have largely remained elite despite the recognition of the importance of increasing participation rates.

The increasing demand for higher education has not been met mainly due to budgetary constraints. The private sector has a role to play in providing higher education programs to the majority of people who in the past could not access higher education. There could be private-public sector co-operation in this area, for example, to use franchise material from the private sector by the public sector, institutions contracting the private sector companies to deliver instruction in their areas of specialty.

One successful story is that of the partnership arrangement between a private company and university in South Africa for first year literacy classes to all students. There is need to encourage and support South to South linkages similar to those promoted through Luced-I &UA for involving higher education institutions directly in development issues. The consortia aims at developing human resources through student, faculty, and researcher exchanges, curriculum development, improved teaching methods, research networking, and joint projects in teaching and research.

It is desirable given the disparities amongst nations and the need to ensure development, that development opportunities should be enabled by the "haves" but be owned by the "have-nots". Africa's new initiative for reconstruction NEPAD is based on the premise that Africans need to take the initiative in their own development. Historically the relations between the North and South economically and politically have been underpinned by a pretense to help developing countries improve their economic situation but resulted in those countries getting poorer. Part of the solution is to let those who need help take ownership of development strategies, revise policies, change economic relationships between the rich and the poor, encourage investment in poor countries.

There is need for genuine commitment to development and mutually beneficial partnership arrangements between institutions in the North and those in the South. There is need at a global level for the development of policies that are enabling for institutions to access technology and information. If such policies are put in place then universities could participate and play their role in development. There is need to rethink the role of higher education in development because it has become part of the enrichment agenda through agencies such as the WTO and GATS arrangements and not part of the development agenda for sustainable development. For globalization to benefit all, there is need to share growth in a more equitable way.

3

Implications of Quality Education

Globalisation refers to the increasing flow of technology, finance, trade, knowledge, people, values, and ideas across borders. Of course, technology, finance, trade, knowledge, people, values, and ideas have been flowing across borders for millennia.

The speed of the transborder flow has constantly increased, with faster methods of transport (of people and equipment) and faster methods of communication (of information and ideas). However, until the last century, we could move information around no faster than we could move people who knew or carried that information. The advent of electronic communication changed that. Now, through radio and television, we can be as immediately informed of a train crash half a world away as one half a mile away. This inculcates a mental orientation that further encourages globalisation. Also, the combination of the affordable personal computer, powerful software packages, and cheap interconnection via world-wide networks has increased the flow of ideas and data by many orders of magnitude. We can now store, retrieve, manipulate and transmit data, representing information, knowledge and ideas. We can do it quickly, conveniently, and in bulk.

Why Globalisation?

Thus, there are mechanisms for globalisation, as defined above, but mechanisms can remain unused if there are no incentives for their use. What are the reasons for globalisation? The reasons are inter-related and cumulative, but they include travel, economics & education.

Travel

Travel has become more convenient and affordable for more people, and in educational institutions, this translates into increased staff and student mobility. This in turn brings with it a desire to have international recognition of credits and qualifications to facilitate travel as a current student or recent graduate.

Free trade zones

Many groups of countries are setting up free trade zones, thereby encouraging the flow of trade and finance across the borders within the zone. The trade leads to the movement of people to support it. They take their knowledge, values and ideas. For education, this means the need to educate people who are comfortable with operating in different racial, ethnic and national environments, and whose qualifications to do so are accepted by the recipients of whatever service they are providing.

Multinational companies

Multinational companies usually wish to be able to employ staff (professionals and other specialists) in different countries with known qualifications; or to move their staff internationally and have the staff's qualifications recognised; or to provide staff development activities wherever the staff maybe be, the results of which must be transferable. This movement is not restricted to free-trade zones.

Education

Following from the above, ways are needed to provide, internationally, information about the nature, level, and quality of education.

Mobility of education

A second educational reason for globalisation is that people learn about the education on offer elsewhere, and want it. This means that the people travel or the education does. There are many ways to achieve the latter, and each has its own characteristics, benefits and drawbacks.

The business of education

Building on these needs, education itself has become an international business. This brief introduction indicates the central role played by education in globalisation.

Education at a Distance

The first clutch of aspects are as follows:

—Transnational education

—On-line education

—Distance education

—Collaborative education

These concepts intersect, and a single educational activity may take two or more of these forms: distance education may or may not be online or transnational; transnational education may or may not be collaborative, etc.

Transnational Education

Transnational education (TNE) denotes any teaching or learning activity in which the students are in a different country (the host country) to that in which the institution providing the education is based (the home country). This situation requires that national boundaries be crossed by information about the education, and by staff and/or educational materials (whether the information and the materials travel by mail, computer network, radio or television broadcast or other means).

This is a response to people's desire for an education offered by an institution abroad, and the institution arranges for the education to be available in their home country. Alternatively, the impetus comes from the institution, seeking markets for its education.

The following are some examples of TNE, to give a flavour of some possibilities. Branch campuses:

campuses set up by an institution in a host country to provide its educational programs to foreign students. Such campuses may be staffed by local people from the host country and/or staff from the home country on short or long-term visits. Franchises: an institution (A) approves an institution (B) in another country to provide one or more of A's programs to students in B's country.

Articulation: the systematic recognition by an institution (A) of specified study at an institution (B) in another country as partial credit towards a program at institution A. Twinning: agreements between institutions in different countries to offer joint programs.

Corporate programs: many large corporations offer programs, principally for their own staff. Where the programs are more extensive and/or form and/or structured, rather than small-scale and possibly ad hoc staff development, the term 'corporate university' is often being used. The programs are sometimes linked with an academic institution so employees can obtain formal and possibly transferable credit for the work. This often involves crediting across national borders.

Distance education programs: those distance education programs that are delivered - through satellites, computers, correspondence, or other technological means - across national boundaries.

A recent survey by IDP of involvement by Australian universities in TNE found that the typical program abroad has, inter alia, the following characteristics.

— In business, administration or economics

— In Hong Kong, Malaysia or Singapore

— four semesters

— involves a local partner that is an education institution

— face-to-face teaching or supported distance learning

— curriculum not adapted to local conditions

— intellectual property owned by home institution

— responsibility for curriculum, teaching assessment and QA with home institution

— responsibility for study location, marketing, financial administration with host institution

On-line Education: the 'Virtual University'

At present there is no generally accepted meaning of the term 'virtual university', or more generally 'virtual institution', but at present it is capturing the absence of a campus with a group of academics located together. Now, not only are the students likely to be in distant locations, but the staff may be too, so the programs are provided and serviced primarily on-line through some form of computer-mediated communications. Furthermore, the staff who develop programs may not be those who support them, and those who assess them may be different again. Without a campus, the institution has been dubbed 'virtual'.

The virtual university builds directly on the widely available computer power and computer networks I identified as mechanisms for globalisation. The options offered to education via the range of information-provision and information-handling techniques may change the whole character of education - or at least, of some of education. The last phrase is an important qualification. The new modes don't mean the end of education as we know it. On the contrary, they may be the saviour we need. We've been trying to do things like increase enrolments, open access, and provide lifelong learning, while using traditional tools, methods and systems not well-suited to these new tasks.

The new modes might enable us actually to do these things. One new aspect is the unbundling of activities assumed to be integrally related to each other and to a place (the campus), such as information provision, admission & registration, program development, study, student support, 'library' access, assessment etc. This unbundling will lead to new models for education.

Distance Education On-line

Many existing 'non-virtual' universities who were not interested in distance education via print or video, are making increasing use of the internet to develop on-line distance education.

Many institutions are taking up on-line education because they envisage economies in staff costs: once a course is created, it can be repeated to indefinite numbers of students without further staff intervention. However, that there may be other benefits for the same costs, such as increased access and internationalisation. In this new environment, existing practices or policies may be inapplicable. Copyright and intellectual property are two issues that have come to the fore with on-line education, as the ability to manipulate and re-combine information has increased. It is worth remembering the term 'flexible learning'. As campus-based institutions are introducing distance options via electronic means (possibly for economy or to serve a new clientele) often they find that the major users are their own campus-based students doing some of their courses on-line.

Universities that are effectively implementing on-line courses also report students appreciation of the high level of interaction with a greater number of other students than usually occurs in face-to-face learning. John Seely Brown of Xerox suggests that we are moving from using technology to support individuals to using technology to support relationships. This will facilitate lifelong learning.

Collaborative Education

In the UK, this tends to mean franchising, and tends to subsume TNE on the grounds that all off-shore operations involve partners. This, however, is a rather restricted interpretation of the concept.

Two models for collaboration in DE in the USA are Western Governors University (WGU) and the Southern Region Education Board's Electronic Campus (SREB). WGU is a virtual institution that offers courses created by about 40 colleges and universities. Started in 1998, it offers a competency-based testing system to achieve its degrees, in competition with existing colleges. It has 950 courses, five degrees, and 200 students. It is seeking accreditation, and this is forcing four US regional accreditation commissions to work together. SREB is a loose collective that started by providing members with little more than a common Internet site on which to advertise their on-line courses.

Also started in 1998, it now lists 3,200 courses and 100 degree programs from 260 institutions. Students earn course credits and degrees from those institutions. SREB has yet to work out an easy credit transfer scheme. Judging by the numbers, the low-key, de-centralised approach seems to have been more successful.

Supping with the devil: academia/business collaboration

Other models for collaboration involve commercial partners. Peter Goodhew reports in a recent THES on what he calls 'Europe's first totally Internet-based global masters degree in IT', which was developed by an English University and an Israeli partner, who set up a Dutch company with the help of two American software providers. Egypt has signed an agreement with VirtualAcademics.com for the company's Barrington University to use satellites to transmit courses in English and computing to Arabic nations. Universitas21 is planning to design courses for presentation via a commercial partner, with degree testamurs listing all the members of U21. This raises quality questions. Will the QAA allow the University of Nottingham to put its name to the testamur unless the course has been through the UK's audit and assessment procedures? Since AUQA is concerned with all academic activities to which an Australian university puts its name, would this mean that AUQA would have to audit U21 when it audits the Universities of Melbourne, Queensland and Sydney? U21 has suggested that the venture permits the universities to earn money from the on-line educational world that will enable them to keep loss-making campuses open. Concerned voices ask what happens to copyright, intellectual property, integrity of courses, and academic freedom if the commercial partner decides that profit-making requires particular steps to be taken.

Mobility and Recognition

One of the flows of globalisation is people. They move to work or study, and this means that they want their study and qualifications accepted in the countries to which they move. In fact, the pressure may be stronger than this. The General Agreement on Trade in Services (GATS) puts a requirement on its signatories that they facilitate the trade in services. This can mean that signatories are required to accept the competence of a consultant educated in another country. Countries within free trade areas (such as the EC, NAFTA, MERCOSUR) have similar requirements stemming from their local agreements.

Recognition of Qualifications

Conventions about the recognition of academic degrees have been signed since 1953 in Europe. As a consequence of these treaties, networks of national agencies for academic recognition (the NARIC and ENIC centres) have been created to deal with the external validation of academic learning. The Lisbon Convention has extended their work, and now places the burden of proof on the recognition authority assessing the qualification, rather than its holder. The Convention also seeks information about the methods of assessing the quality of institutions and programs. Australia is active in signing mutual recognition agreements, either bilaterally or via APEC.

Increasing mobility of students, either mid-course or to a subsequent course, is putting increasing pressure on institutional admissions officers, who find they have to use a great variety of information sources. There is scope here for a 'database of everything', of that would capture information on all quality agencies and all approved courses at all accredited institutions. We need accurate, up-to-date information on the nature and status of institutions, and the meaning of the qualifications they offer. Such an extensive information bank might be beyond our capabilities, even with the current information handling technology. The main difficulty might prove to be the manual step of keeping the information complete and current.

Employability

These recognition systems do not link intellectual power to employability, and European ministers signed the Sorbonne Declaration and the Bologna Declaration to push the development of a European HE Area, and point away from academic recognition towards competence appraisal. The Bologna Declaration calls for the 'promotion of European co-operation in QA with a view to developing comparable criteria and methodologies'. Active discussion throughout Europe is now taking place to set down some basic ideas about the outcomes of HE in European countries. It is leading to greater interest in accreditation, and harmonisation of external QA processes across Europe.

The Role of Professional Associations

Attention to the mobility of professionals has given a fillip to professional accrediting associations, whose members are demanded international collaboration between associations in order to achieve international recognition of the professional qualifications. The most-cited development in this field is the 'Washington

Accord' between the Institutions of Professional Engineers in eight countries, agreeing that:

— the criteria, policies and procedures used by the signatories in accrediting engineering academic programs are comparable; and

— the accreditation decisions rendered by one signatory are acceptable to the other signatories.

Two other countries are on the verge of joining. This gives engineering graduates a high level of mobility. Despite the wide attention to this Accord, it has not spawned many copies. This may be because the engineering associations are associations that 'belong to' their members, and people do not have to belong in order to be allowed legally to call themselves 'engineer'. Professions more tightly controlled by law or statute are finding the mutual recognition task more difficult.

Contradictions

We can note contrary tendencies in this area:

i. increasing rigidity, as countries seek to harmonise structures, eg degree length, learning frameworks, to permit mobility and recognition

ii. increasing flexibility, with more emphasis on outcomes, and/or equivalence at a more basic level - 'substantial equivalence'.

Trade in Education

Not long ago, the international movement of students or

education was seen as either for mutual benefit between equals, or for the purposes of aid to less wealthy or developed countries. Although these aspects have not entirely disappeared, these movements are now firmly in the basket of international trade. This brings into sharper focus such considerations as consumer protection and cultural impact. It also means that education falls within the sphere of GATS, and a country signing the agreement without making explicit reservations at the time of signing can find that it is required to accept from beyond its borders courses and providers about which it has some reservations. Various Codes of Practice have been drawn up to address this. The GATE Principles for TNE were written with a very strong consumer protection focus. Cultural impact is much more difficult to handle. One way is to require that courses be adapted to match the needs and nature of the society in the host country, but sometimes students do not want such an adaptation, and sometimes the provider uses the adaptation to provide a cut-down course. Other Codes of Practice address the treatment of students who have travelled to study in the institution's home country.

Implications for Quality

At the 1991 INQAAHE conference, Malcolm Fraser said that the 90s would be the decade of quality. It may be that the 00s (the noughties?!) will be the decade of international quality. To support globalisation, educational institutions are paying increasing attention to internationalisation, which is the process of integrating an international / intercultural dimension into the teaching, research and service functions of the institution. As institutions internationalise their curricula or their research links, or offer courses abroad or enrol foreign students, all these activities should be subject to internal QA processes. By the same token, external QA agencies must be able to assess the nature and effect of these internal processes. This is the process of 'QA of internationalisation'. Where competence in QA in this area does not exist (whether internally or externally), it must be developed.

A similar phrase with a different meaning is 'internationalisation of QA'. Most QA agencies started as national agencies, but globalisation and internationalisation of HE mean that increasingly, QA agencies must be able to operate internationally. Examples of international operation by QA agencies include:

— A QA agency follows its institutions' courses abroad (which could be done in several ways, such as sending review panels abroad, or checking at a distance (electronically or otherwise), or contracting another body (eg another QA agency) to carry out the check).

— A QA agency takes responsibility for everything that happens in its region, so it checks educational imports at the border

— A QA agency recognises the activities carried out and decisions reached by another QA agency abroad.

— There is a global 'certifying' agency, which can check and certify the quality of QA agencies themselves .

— There is a global 'accrediting' agency, which can check and accredit any institution (perhaps by recognising the results of the check carried out by the relevant national agency).

A Global Accreditor

EUA

For several years, EUA has been offering an audit service to its members. This has been very popular, as universities choose the scope of the audit to best suit their needs, and the audit becomes a management consultancy carried out by people who have been part of academic management. There has been criticism of a conservative approach—possibly due to having panels comprising former rectors. It operates on a cost-recovery basis.

IQR

The IMHE of the OECD developed, and now offers together with EUA and ACA, an audit of an institution's processes and progress in internationalisation (Knight & de Wit, 1999). This is at an early stage of its operation, and it remains to be seen how popular and useful it will be. There is s slight tension between whether it is an audit against the institution's own objectives in internationalisation, or against the definition given above.

GATE

In 1995, the Global Alliance for Transnational Education (GATE) was established to address issues relating to the quality of educational offerings that cross national boundaries. It drafted Principles (a code of practice) to which HE institutions should adhere in these activities, and set up a process for certifying institutional adherence to the Principles.

A general purpose accreditor

Many enquiries to GATE came from institutions wanting, not a review of their TNE, but a broad-scope review of their academic quality and standards. There is room for an agency that will offer such a service, and discussions continue on the best approach to establishing such a body. It would be of great value to institutions that want to feature on the international scene, but which are in countries where there is no QA agency, or the QA agency does not have a high international reputation.

Mutual Recognition of the Activities of QA Agencies

The Washington Accord that provides mutual recognition of the actions of eight accrediting agencies. INQAAHE is the only vehicle linking national accreditors world-wide. Full Membership is open only to bona fide QA agencies, and applicants' procedures are checked to ensure they satisfy this criterion before admission. However, the check is only on paper, and no attempt is made to investigate the substance, nor the implementation of the proclaimed procedures. Therefore, membership of INQAAHE is not a sanction of the member's procedures.

The reason for this approach is that INQAAHE was established for mutual support and information sharing. In this situation, a QA agency that is not operating very well can still benefit from membership, and does not detract from INQAAHE by being a member. However, INQAAHE could tighten the membership requirement, in the sense of carrying out a fuller check of the prospective member's operations. Then, INQAAHE membership would be the organisational equivalent of an engineer or lawyer being a member of his or her professional association, which has checked its members' credentials before admission. In this situation, INQAAHE could be a vehicle for mutual recognition of qualifications, as INQAAHE membership would provide a guarantee of the performance of the QA that has accredited the institution (using that term loosely) that has granted the qualification.

Even without the INQAAHE Board imposing more restrictive conditions for membership, which could be considered unhelpful, exclusive, or impractical, more formal links can be established between members to facilitate this mutual recognition of qualifications. An INQAAHE Action Group is trying May to take forward the thinking and discussion on Mutual Recognition of QA agencies.

There are a great many thorny questions in this area. For example, can an agency that reviews at program level and one that reviews at institution level meaningfully recognise each other's activities? Autonomous institutions are not bound to give credit to a student for work done at another institution that answers to the same accreditor. Therefore, even if two agencies accept the other's activities as valid and rigorous, will it have any effect on what their respective institutions will accept?

A Quality Hallmark

Another INQAAHE Action Group is working on the concept of a quality hallmark for QA agencies. A 'quality hallmark' would need a Code of Good Practice for QA agencies, and possibly then an independent body to certify to this code. Such a process would be analogous to that used in the general QA world, where organisations can be accredited to certify to standards such as ISO 9000. The proposal under discussion by INQAAHE for an international Hallmark proposes the following criteria:

— The mission and vision of the agency are clearly formulated and made public

— The agency has competent and qualified staff

— The agency has a system to assure its own quality, and is itself periodically reviewed

— The agency's work draws on the services of competent and qualified people.

— The agency's protocols for institutional self-assessment and for the agency's subsequent external assessment are clearly stated and firmly adhered to

— The methods for setting standards (for processes and outcomes) are open

— The criteria used for making judgments are clear and public.

— The assessment is a regular and cyclical activity

— The assessment is carried out by an independent group, panel or committee, and stakeholders have no influence on the judgment

— The assessment addresses the most important aspects

— There is a public, in some form that permits public understanding of the quality and standards assessed.

Clearly there are problems in getting international agreement on such a protocol, from the philosophical (what constitutes independence?) to the practical (can we apply the same process to a program-review and an institutional-review agency?) Nonetheless, meta-evaluation - ie evaluation of the evaluators - is a major priority:

— Note the theme of the 1999 INQAAHE conference.

— Note the recent THES headlines about the total explicit and implicit, external and internal cost of the external review processes.

With the possible exception of the US regional accrediting agencies, no external QA agency has been set up by institutions totally voluntarily. Either they are set up by governments, or by the institutions because the latter fear the government is going to set one up. In a similar vein, QA agency colleagues rather conservative. They talk about the difficulties of mutual recognition; they baulk at the idea that anyone may judge them for the purposes of giving them a quality stamp and find them wanting. But they may find that the world has flowed on, and marooned them on their island. As I've already noted, governments are pushing the issue of mutual recognition; QA agencies are sometimes disparaging of the NARIC-type recognition community, but it is the latter that are at the sharp end of making judgments that can make or break an individual's profession; professional agencies are moving faster, but again because of the pressure of free trade agreements and the clamour by their members for mechanisms to facilitate their mobility.

As the new flexibility increases the variety of educational programs and providers, QA systems aligned to conventional modes may be a force for conservatism. If so, they will be ignored by employers and governments or bypassed by new structures. A more profitable evolution is to develop appropriate guarantees for the new modes.

The Flexible QA Agency

One consequence of globalisation is an enormous amount of activity in the QA world, much of it beyond the capacity of individual institutions, and much outside the purview of the QA agency as usually conceived. This suggests that the responsibility for action should be spread more widely. Unfortunately, if something is everyone's responsibility, it may be no-one's responsibility, so there may always be need for some 'agency' or 'body' to check what steps are being taken and how effective they are, but it may not need to look much like an EQA agency as we currently conceive it. In the commercial world, organisations with strong internal auditing practices are negotiating with their certifying body alternative EQA arrangements to rationalise costs and simplify the process. Audit sampling and self-surveillance audits witnessed by the certification body are being implemented by several organisations. HE needs to move in the same direction.

The 'external quality manager' (EQM) could be a body that interacts with institutions and operates by monitoring, reviewing and validating the peer and other activities of institutions and other agencies (Woodhouse, 2000). Mechanisms it might use at institution level include:

— Audit by the EQM

— Evidence from international benchmarking

— Validation by international consortia

— Accreditation by foreign accreditors
— Accreditation by validating institutions (eg the CVU members)
— Accreditation by international accreditors
— Evidence from the achievement of quality awards
— Evidence from ISO 9000 certification

Mechanisms it could use in relation to programs and qualifications include:

— The EQM's own program approval function. This would assist institutions that want a single body to actually carry out all their external quality activities.
— Program work could be 'subcontracted' to other bodies, with the EQM auditing the program approval operations of its 'subcontractors'
— The EQM may permit institutions to approve their own programs ('self-accreditation') subject to EQM audits of the procedures. This would assist institutions with well-developed and secure internal processes.
— Evidence from international benchmarking
— Institutions could undertake a system-wide program-level, discipline-oriented review (cf The Netherlands)
— Validation by international consortia
— Certification by international accreditors
— Evidence from ISO 9000 certification
— Evidence from professional association accreditation

The EQM could further customise the procedure by taking account of the academic maturity of an institution in determining the scope, stringency and frequency of audits of the institution and its program-level activities. Our mental image is always of a one-to-one relation between the QA agency and each of its institutions. Perhaps we should move on from this and encourage more interaction between institutions (whether in formal consortia or informal clusters), with the EQM relating to groups of institutions. Taking this further, perhaps the emphasis on the inter-institutional interaction should be on benchmarking, with the detailed management-level parameters being shared between the institutions, but the more global descriptive parameters being revealed to the EQM(s). If the institutional cluster spans various EQM jurisdictions, the agencies should co-operate in their interaction with the group.

Partly as a consequence of globalisation, matters that are now envisaged when the word 'quality' is used are very wide-ranging, from academic excellence through national development to international recognition. It is time to take a more flexible approach to our concepts of quality, qualifications, quality assurance, and mutual recognition. QA agencies or EQMs will become less direct checkers of quality and more orchestrators and gatherers and authenticators of evidence from a wide variety of sources. Their integrity will be essential, but other things will be less important. For example, it should not matter whether institutions or government own it, provided they trust it.

Universities in the New Global Economy

The Role of Universities in the New Global Economy is a vast topic and one which can be analysed from several perspectives, as the organizers have recognized by identifying a number of sub-themes to be addressed and thus broadening the panel's collective focus. It invites us to look at the 'big picture' even if we all know that vast differences exist on the ground between and within different regions and countries in the world. Also, universities are only one set of actors even within the educational universe. They are part of an increasingly diversified higher education sector and their unique role needs now to be examined and defined in the context of the other institutional contributions. But when the focus is on universities, it must be underlined that it is precisely their wider and more comprehensive societal role that defines their specificity in this new landscape.

The increased and often almost exclusive focus on the university as a driver of economic development, could threaten that specificity by undermining some of the basic values for which the university stands and which it is expected to uphold and pass on. This is not to say that universities do not play a major role in local and regional economic development, particularly in the South. However, there too, the broader contributions that universities make to society must be recognized, encouraged and protected. The search for alternatives and new paths to sustainable development are important in all regions of the world and require broad-based, general education developing the analytical, soft skills so needed in a world full of complexity and contradiction. This was a key message of Peril and Promise, a report of the World Bank/UNESCO Task Force of 1997.

The World Bank's own latest strategy, entitled Constructing Knowledge Societies, now underlines the social, public role and broad societal benefits of tertiary education, which include greater social cohesion, improved health, better basic and secondary education, democratic participation etc. As well, while taking the macro view, we need to exercise caution with the other half of the overall title for our session. The assumption that there is a New Global Economy also requires some caveats since many of the Least Developed Countries in particular, are not integrated into this global economy, whether new or old, on an equal footing.

Internationalization or globalization of higher education?

Coming from the International Association of Universities, my comments will focus on the internationalization of higher education on the one hand, and the impact on higher education of the forces of globalization on the other. This is fitting because IAU's existence and mandate for more than 50 years have rested on the premise that international cooperation among universities and more recently internationalization of higher education, offer solid paths towards better and stronger universities, in a more just and peaceful world. Today globalization of the higher education sector is radically changing even the way it is internationalizing by creating a new and complex dynamic.

The full extent of the changes that globalization of higher education may bring is still largely unpredictable and may remain so for some time. But already the debate is on about its threatening or negative aspects, as well as about the positive opportunities that it may offer. Indeed, higher education is both a major driver of economic growth through its teaching and research functions, and simultaneously, higher education is an economic sector itself, a huge one, representing millions of dollars or Euros in each country and billions internationally as a service sector being exchanged or traded. As this sector continues to globalize, many argue that here too, we must beware of the fact that those who are doing the globalizing may reap its benefits while those who are being globalized may be subject to far less positive consequences.

All of us are searching for a better understanding of the interconnected forces that are transforming societies, forces of a technological, economic, political and social nature. And in this search, very broad but often undefined concepts such as globalization, knowledge society, sustainable development, public good and even internationalization, have become shorthand in our higher education discourse in the last few years. Yet, to really explore what is happening and to do so in an international context, with the intercultural and linguistic dimensions as addional layers of meaning, it is critical to start by articulating what we mean by the words we use. We may not all agree. However, at least the areas of disagreement will become clearer and that too is essential for a dialogue or debate.

Internationalization

Internationalization as a pro-active effort on the part of universities to embrace their universal nature by opening their curriculum, their research, their classrooms and networks to the world. It means introducing an international dimension into how we teach and what we learn, what we expect from our faculty members and who we hope to attract to our classrooms, laboratories and as partners in our research projects. However, in the fifteen years or so internationalization has been adopted as a strategic goal, and in many universities, pursued through specific policies and actions at every level.

This has been so in large measure due to an acceleration of economic globalization, which in turn was greatly facilitated by an explosion of information and communications technologies. In that respect, internationalization can be viewed as an initial response to these trends by many universities. Many among them opened international relations offices, designed new programs, institutionalized their international research networks and began, in earnest, to pay attention to how they exposed students to the shrinking outside world which required such exposure and understanding. The main characteristics of this process include an emphasis on academic mobility and two-way exchange both of students and faculty, international research projects and networks, more academic courses integrating an international perspective and a greater emphasis on how international cooperation projects particularly with developing country universities are mutually enriching for all participants. Internationalization in this sense has an academic and cultural rationale first, with the entrepreneurial dimension, present but some where in the back seat.

Globalization and higher education

Change is rarely linear or sequential and the globalization of higher education as a sector of the economy is taking place simultaneously, in response to some of the same external forces, manifesting itself in similar actions but with somewhat different institutional motivations and consequences. These processes are complimentary but different and their respective consequences are rather difficult to untangle. To do so is essential though, especially for policy-making to reinforce the positive and diminish the negative impacts. Globalization of higher education and demonstrate more through examples than a definition. In this process, higher education is viewed as an economic sector with some of its institutions acting globally as large multinationals. They are delocalizing, franchising, exporting places by importing students, designing global marketing strategies to increase these exports, selling consulting services and setting up profit centres which generate revenues for further development, building international alliances and networks etc.

Universities are capitalizing on their brand name recognition and whole countries are doing so in order to either protect their overseas market share, as is the case for the US, Australia, \the UK and to some extent Canada, which have so far enjoyed the lion's share. Others are just entering the scene and want to win a share of that market as newcomers. Here we see governments of Germany, the Netherlands and France among others, elaborating major initiatives to ensure that their institutions occupy part of this global market space. This process too is about retaining excellence and strength in higher education. Some would say it is about survival in the context of the following external factors:

1. The reality of a knowledge-based economy in which producing, disseminating, adapting, using and applying knowledge are the key factors of economic growth and competitiveness;

2. Declining real per student funding from public sources, despite the overall growth of the sector and in direct contrast to the rhetorical importance given to knowledge and higher education by governments;
3. An increasingly regionalized but also globalized labour market, and of course,
4. The ICT revolution.

All of these factors act as push-pull levers on individual institutions and on the system as a whole. In the knowledge-based economy, global demand for higher education is steadily growing. The most important fact though is that this represents a 90% increase since 1970. For higher education, UNESCO data allow her to estimate a total of 88 million students world-wide and the vast majority in publicly funded universities. Furthermore, these numbers are still far from meeting the demand for higher education and so further expansion is likely. In fact, Denis Blight, former head of IDP in Australia estimated several years ago that in Asia alone, the demand for higher education would grow by 48 million students between 1995 and 2020. This he equated to a need for 37,000 new university places each week. John Daniel, then Vice Chancellor of the Open University in the UK, writing in Mega Universities and Knowledge Media published in 1996 projected the global need for one university per week. What other sector of the economy projects this kind of growth in demand?

This growing demand for higher education is coupled with an almost chronic funding crisis in public higher education. Perhaps the most dramatic case of this has been the UK since the 1980s, but in almost all OECD countries, decline of per student funding as a percentage of GDP per capita has been case. For most governments, there is an expectation that university funding must become more diversified. In some systems this means an increasing share covered by students. In other systems, particularly where tuition remains free, these reductions are to be met by efficiency gains, streamlining and increased revenue generation. The result more generally has been a growing and fierce competition for funds, for faculty who will attract research funds, for students and for service contracts for training and consultancies, in short, competition for a share of the education and training market at home and increasingly world-wide.

The entrepreneurial aspect has moved from the back seat to share the front of the bus. A second consequence has been, an explosion of new private providers both 'not for profit' and 'for profit', in many higher education systems whether these systems are predominantly publicly funded or whether they already have a healthy private higher education system. Even within the public sector, commodification of higher education is becoming a reality. The inclusion of trade in educational services in the GATS is but the most stark example of this new reality but by no means the only one. The regional and even global labour market, particularly for academics, researchers and scientists, and for students as well, is another key facilitator of higher education globalization. Projections for teacher and faculty shortages in countries such as Canada, the US and elsewhere, as well the competition for other professionals, for example in the health field, are giving rise to policies to retain, attract and import highly qualified people.

The concept of Brain Drain, is now used in the context of intra-OECD competition for the best brains. It has been dusted off and has served as a lever to stimulate R&D investment in several countries. Yet, these policies also have a debilitating impact where the Brain Drain has been a reality for some time. The World Bank indicates that already in 1990, 75% of all emigrants from sub-Saharan Africa and 75% of all those from India were holders of tertiary education qualifications.

The European Union offers a good example of such 'import' strategies. In both its educational programming, such as with the renown ERASMUS program, and in the research field with the 6th Framework Programme's Marie Curie grants, the EU is planning to launch well-funded, world-wide opportunities to allow non-EU students and scientists to come to European institutions. The likelihood that some of these individuals extend their stay in the host country is fairly high in light of the conditions that are being proposed. This does not appear to worry the EU policy-makers. The fourth and final factor, needs no real elaboration. The application of ICTs to teaching and learning, which have caused a veritable explosion of distance education and e-learning opportunities, coupled with the other factors mentioned, create totally unprecedented transformations in the higher educational scene within nation states and at the transnational level. The now widely-used term 'borderless education' is appropriate not only for cross border or international delivery of education by means of traditional in-class methods. ICTs when applied to education also remove the frontiers imposed by time and physical distance.

The dual development through ICTs, of new 'virtual' or e-learning institutions, and technology enhanced learning opportunities offered by almost every traditional university add new potential for globalizing the system for all higher education actors. The cumulative effect of these factors on the higher education systems and institutions means that to varying degrees they have become characterized by increasing diversification of types of institutions, programs, delivery channels and students or clients, greater privatization and perhaps most importantly by the highly competitive nature of the environment.

Internationally, other countries are viewed in terms of market potential rather than as partners whose academics may have insights into a discipline or research project and will add an international dimension. In this process, using English is a real asset since it makes programs accessible to many more. There is less concern that the use of English may be a threat to cultural diversity and a factor for homogenizing the educational offer. It must be noted that higher education internationalization and globalization are not mutually exclusive phenomena, nor do they represent opposing poles on a continuum as these comments may have led you believe. In fact, they can often be indistinguishable and the promotion of one can strengthen the occurrence of the other.

Yet, they do differ in goals and long-term results. For this reason, it is crucial not to \use these terms as interchangeable. The realm of globalization is the market place; its motor is most often, if not always, economic and it is fueled by competition. Institutions build alliances within and across systems and strive to fill a niche more than to fulfill a need. Internationalization is less market-oriented and depends more on policies and incentives that are academic rather than economic in nature. For this reason, cooperation, two-way exchange and partnerships predominate in these relations. Both trends are present in today's higher education system worldwide. Both are having an incredibly dynamic influence on higher education systems and institutions and are profoundly changing the domestic and international landscape giving rise to many new providers, new delivery mechanisms, new kinds of linkages and networks among institutions of higher learning but also with the business community. The challenges ahead are many. But a priority must be on finding the appropriate balance between the pressures to internationalize academically and the need to remain an active player in the globalized system.

This requires finding ways to ensure that the potential negative impacts such as homogenization, exclusion of some individuals or parts of the world from the opportunities offered by this new dynamic, excessive commodification and privatization of higher education, etc. are countered by the political will to recognize higher education as a public good and by policies that promote international cooperation and capacity building rather than increased exports. At the same time, it is becoming apparent that in this world of globalized higher education, a new infrastructure is needed for sharing information, for collective advocacy, for identifying and addressing gaps such as adequate quality assurance and regulatory mechanisms to protect the learners.

This regulatory policy infrastructure needs to be developed by the higher education community working collectively rather than by the market working through WTO rule s. As actors and spectators in both internationalization and globalization pro cesses and mindful of the different impact actions have whether we are doing the globalizing or are being globalized, universities may need to ask themselves some of the questions proposed below, as they develop international initiatives. These may be helpful in advancing the analysis of the longer term and unintended impacts of internationalization and globalization of higher education.

Whether as Actors or as Spectators in the New Global Economy, universities have a tremendous responsibility towards society to continue to search for answers and to find the appropriate balance between the various and often contradictory forces pulling at them. It seems to me that IAU too can play a role in collaboration with regional university organizations in Europe, Africa and elsewhere to build this new international infrastructure that will help ensure that many reap the benefits of a strong global higher education system.

4

Universities in Globalisation

The term 'globalization', covers a vast number of interpretations and generates emotional and often not very rational reactions, to the point of becoming a problem in itself. It is important that universities develop a better definition of this concept and share it with their students and society as a whole. Globalization is neither the supreme monster, the cause of all problems which must be destroyed at all costs, nor is it the unique and ideal path towards prosperity, a path which should be followed blindly.

In its current form, globalization has many positive aspects which must be promoted: for example, direct access to unfiltered and uncensored information thanks to the Internet. However, it also has very negative aspects which must be changed. For example, its analytical framework is focused too narrowly on financial considerations and not enough on cultural and social considerations and it also leads to growing disparities between countries and even between citizens of the same country. Globalization is a phenomenon that offers humanity problems as well as opportunities, a phenomenon which must be studied, understood and managed so that it will lead to a global interdependence and generate progress that is equitable for all nations and all citizens of the world. As John Daniel rightly reminded us, referring to the state of the world economy in the early 20th century, globalization is not as new a phenomenon for our societies and the world economy as we would like to think. It is certainly not new for universities.

Indeed, globalization has always been an integral part of university life, ever since Bologna University was created and its members were granted safe conduct by Emperor Frédéric Barberousse to move freely within medievál Europe. Moreover, John Daniel reminded us of the examples of Erasmus, a professor known throughout the great universities of Europe at the time, and of those unruly English students who created Oxford University after being expelled from the Sorbonne.

We need only recall the international mobility of researchers that has always existed, the role of international learned societies in all disciplines of knowledge, and the role of academic journals and large international conferences as preferred means to disseminate research results; all of this is proof that the practice of globalization is well established in academic communities.

However, what is new is the extent of the current phenomenon of globalization, that is, the growing interdependence of all societies and all segments of each society; the accelerating pace of movement of ideas, goods and people; the emergence of the phenomenon of local decisions having a global impact; the increasing complexity and uncertainty of the world and its mechanisms; and of course, the impact of the Internet whose effects we are barely beginning to grasp. We need to better understand the consequences of this evolution so that we can adapt to it, but also and especially, so that we can master it and guide it in a direction that is conducive to the progress of all humanity. The fact that the world is evolving towards globalization poses two types of problems for higher education: problems related to our teaching and research mission - how to adapt our teaching programs, which new research fields to open - and problems linked with our organization and our institutional policies and strategies.

Training and Research Programmes

Of all the issues facing us and which were brought up in this conference, like to consider three in particular.

i) Educational institutions have the dual mission to develop and transmit knowledge and universal values and, at the same time, to contribute to the cultural, economic and social development of the local societies which they serve and which support them. Thus, for each university, the challenge is to find the right balance between these two sometimes contradictory missions. This challenge is all the greater since it must be taken up in a context where knowledge is recognized as a factor critical to economic development and thus regarded by governments and all social players as a means to ensure a competitive advantage to any nation in a globalized world. Universities are thus subject to contradictory pressures: on the one hand, their internal tradition of "scientific communism" encourages them to be open to all exchanges of ideas and people internationally; and, on the other hand, governments and society provide the bulk of their financial resources and expect a return on this investment in the form of contribution to local economic development. In the coming years, finding the right balance between our universal and local missions will be an ever more daunting task.

ii) The world of higher education is still living under the "tyranny" of scientific disciplines and sub-disciplines. "Mode 1" governs our internal structures of faculties and departments, our external structures of knowledge diffusion (learned societies, academic journals), our practices of meritocratic recognition (criteria for hiring and promotion, remuneration of professors, academic awards and distinctions), and our teaching and research programs.

Nevertheless, the problems facing humanity are increasingly complex and transdisciplinary. As pointed out by Michael Gibbons and several other participants, there is an urgent need to adapt to "Mode 2" of knowledge production by introducing an increasing transdisciplinary dimension into our practices. These should include:

— new programs and new structures that are flexible, transdisciplinary and centred on problem solving;

— new systems for recognizing merit, for both professors and institutions, which would put less emphasis on disciplinary merits and give more importance to multi- and inter-disciplinary contributions; and

— new programs, or new activities within existing programs, to give our students greater access to the transdisciplinary dimensions and, hence, a training that is more in keeping with the demands of the complex world in which they live.

iii) the mission of higher education is to train tomorrow's social actors and leaders. These people will have to work in an increasingly complex world and deal with more and more complicated problems. Our programs must be adapted so as to better prepare them to take up this challenge by developing their new capacities:

— learning to learn;

— understanding global and transdisciplinary issues;

— interacting with different social groups: specialists in all fields, citizens often not equipped to understand complex issues, legislators, etc.

— understanding and capacity to act in varied cultural environments; it is by developing students' international mobility, and especially North-South mobility, that this capacity will be most effectively developed; and

— more generally, simultaneous acquisition of universal values and functional and professional knowledge of high quality.

Adaptation of our institutions

Not only does globalization have a major impact on all universities, but this impact is felt in many ways. Six key points have given below:

i) The Internet is radically transforming access to information. The traditional roles of a university professor as a source of knowledge and of the campus as the unique place for the transmission of this knowledge are being strongly challenged. While we can certainly attempt to resist this evolution, it would be at our own risk. I think that we must, on the contrary, embrace the Internet and adapt to it in several ways.

— Refocusing the role of university professors as mentor, advisor, and guide to students in the search, analysis, criticism and integration of the information available on the Web and elsewhere: this role is vital and must be developed given, as we all know, the amount of nonsense which co-exists with quality information on the Web.

— Following the example of MIT, using the Internet to disseminate quality academic material freely and to the broadest public possible: we must be aware that this approach, which is entirely consistent with our tradition of free movement of ideas, will also open up our pedagogical material to an informal but global system of peer assessment, with all the consequences that this may have for the reputation of professors as well as institutions.

— Using the Internet as a means to considerably increase co-operation between universities and to facilitate new research partnerships: the benefits for universities in countries of the South could be quite substantial.

ii) Globalization and the accelerating knowledge production require that universities rapidly increase their delivery of continuing education programs. However, with a few notable exceptions, universities have generally made little effort in this area.

Continuing education must be integrated into the university's central missions rather than being confined, as is too often the case, to parallel if not external structures. The Internet provides us with an extraordinary tool to deliver, everywhere and "just-in-time," updated knowledge to our graduates to help them deal with career shifts and new professional challenges. Continuing education is a highly competitive business field in which most of the new higher education players are found, including for-profit organisations. Therefore, universities must clearly define their fields of action in order to be successful in this competitive environment. They should probably concentrate on their fundamental mission to develop knowledge and people by providing continuing education to their graduates and not sticking to commercial or financial criteria only.

iii) The main concern of the international academic community should be to fight against the widening of the knowledge gap between developed and emerging nations, so as to prevent the creation of what Teboho Moja called "global apartheid." Many colleagues have emphasized the potential benefits but also the great dangers associated with the growth of interventions by foreign suppliers of higher education services in developing countries. The issues raised by our colleagues Moja and Mohamedbhai should be carefully examined, especially the danger that these foreign stakeholders will objectively prevent local institutions from being developed by creating unfair competition in the recruitment of professors.

New forms of university co-operation must be established. In particular, Michael Gibbons' proposal to develop "twinning" between universities of the North and the South deserves careful consideration as long as everybody agrees that there would be a potential for concrete and much more effective development than that in the co-operation models implemented thus far by the large international organizations. UNESCO and our international associations could play a constructive role in developing this approach.

iv) The issue of funding higher education is extremely complex and unfortunately does not have a simple solution. A further issue is to determine how to share out these financial resources among the various social players - students, governments (and through them the general public), and businesses. Unfortunately, this latter issue has tended to monopolize most political debates, with misinformation often contributing to its superficiality. We must refocus our discussions on the vital issue of the means necessary to deliver quality higher education and on the best ways to ensure wide as well as equal accessibility to all those who have the ability and the desire to acquire a university education and then to contribute effectively to societal development. We must also try to be objective and rigorous in this debate so as to avoid the pitfalls of demagogy.

v) Competitive approaches to relations between universities are probably more harmful than beneficial, if they are assessed in terms of our traditional values of the free movement of ideas and people. We have seen how competition for students, professors and managers contributes to the brain drain and the widening gap between countries of the North and the South, that is, it worsens a situation which we should instead be attempting to put right. Of course, there are outstanding successes such as that of the University of Phoenix in a well-defined field of action, but at the same time there are many failures that are just as noteworthy. If we truly want to protect the traditional values of higher education, i.e. the free movement of ideas and people and the contribution to the production of universal knowledge for the benefit of all humanity, we must chart the course of our actions based on these values, that is, on co-operative rather than competitive approaches.

vi) This leads us to the central issue of higher education and the GATS agreements. We have established a very clear consensus that higher education is not merchandise whose international trade should be regulated according to the same mechanisms as the trade in wood, petroleum or planes. This does not mean that higher education should be excluded from all global trade regulation systems, but rather it should be governed by its own specific system of rules.

The fundamental aspects of globalization as we are experiencing it today; this is a matter for serious thought in the medium and long term. Nevertheless, we must deal with an immediate situation in which, as was succinctly pointed out by Madeleine Green and Eva Egron-Polack, the GATS negotiations were developed between governments without universities having made their positions on the issue known. The academic communities urgently need to take charge of this matter and make their positions known to their government representatives in order to avoid inadvertent but irreparable mistakes.

To formulate these positions, we must seriously examine all aspects of the issue. This has begun in various places, but we must intensify our efforts by using the joint declaration adopted in September 2001 by the Association of Universities and Colleges of Canada, the American Council on Education, the European University Association and the Council for Higher Education Accreditation. However, "nature abhors a vacuum." This is also true of the international community. It is not enough for us to say that "we do not want the GATS." We must say how we want to organize the international space of higher education. No doubt, our collective authorities - IAU, AUC, AUF - have a role to play in this. UNESCO can also play a role by helping us set up an international space based on the principles of free movement of ideas and people, of contribution to the production of universal knowledge, of participation in the process of acculturation of people, and of the cultural, economic and social development of societies which are served by the universities.

Improve the capacity of higher education to contribute to the process of a globalization that is harnessed to achieve a more balanced and equitable development of the living conditions for all citizens of the world.

Universities in the Era of Globalisation

The present capitalism is based on the exploitation of scientific communism'. That is an elegant way of expressing a tension that has always been part of academic life, but which seems more acute today, namely the tension between knowledge as a common good and knowledge as private property. That is also the question put to us by the organisers of this colloquium. 'How do international institutions see higher education issues in a time of accelerating globalisation? Are we headed down the road to mercantilism, or are we moving toward human sustainable development, which acknowledges the world of higher education as having the status of a global public good?' It is a tendentious question anyway, because it expresses a false dichotomy and offers an artificial choice. Let me begin by examining the principles that guide UNESCO in its approach to education in general and to higher education in particular.

The first observation is that it would be hypocritical for UNESCO to oppose the globalisation of education, because the introduction to the Convention that established UNESCO at the end of the Second World War is a plea for globalisation, even though the word did not exist in 1945. We read there:

> That the wide diffusion of culture, and the education of humanity for justice and liberty and peace are indispensable to the dignity of man and constitute a sacred duty which all the nations must fulfil in a spirit of mutual assistance and concern.

For these reasons, the States Parties to this Constitution, believing in full and equal opportunities for education for all, in the unrestricted pursuit of objective truth, and in the free exchange of ideas and knowledge, are agreed and determined to develop and increase the means of communication between their peoples and to employ these means for the purposes of mutual understanding and a truer and more perfect knowledge of each other's lives. There are three ideas in this extract from the UNESCO constitution:

— 'the unrestricted pursuit of objective truth';

— 'the free exchange of ideas and knowledge'; and

— 'increasing the means of communication between peoples'.

These three ideas define a healthy vision of the globalisation of intellectual life and echo the evolution of the academic dogma, the academic mode of thinking and the principle of academic freedom over eight centuries. By academic dogma mean the simple statement that knowledge is important. It is a dogma, because you cannot prove it, but many believe that it is a basic tenet of humankind. By the academic mode of thinking the appeal to reason, the formulation of hypotheses, the search for evidence—in short, the scientific method in the broadest sense.

By academic freedom, to quote the conclusions of a conference organised by UNESCO in 1950, the 'right and the freedom to research science for its own sake, wherever that research leads, the tolerance of opposite views and independence of any political interference'. Are these values under threat today? Should we be erecting barricades to defend the vision of intellectual globalisation set out in UNESCO's constitution? Last year the UNESCO Courier devoted an issue to this question with the title Politics and profit:

Scholars at Risk. It stressed, of course, the difficulties encountered by academics in countries whose regimes tolerate neither opposition nor freedom of speech. But most of the articles were about the dangers created by large firms that fund work in universities. This funding often includes tight restrictions, either on the publication of research results or, more generally, on the research activities of the department in receipt of the funds. The authors quote cases where university authorities kowtowed only too readily to commercial pressures. They explained that universities were turning to the private sector for support because of the decline in the public funding of universities in many countries. There are two comments about this issue.

— Preventing the publication of research results is a shortsighted policy, especially for any organisation that hopes to take advantage of scientific progress. Restrictions on academic freedom only hinder the circulation of knowledge and therefore bias the judgements that countries make and the actions that they take'. Self criticism and self correction are all too rare in human affairs. They are the sign of a maturity and of a spiritual force which provide hope for the future'. In summary, such restrictions are ineffective in commercial terms and are a drag on human progress. Some examples of restrictions on the publication of research results on new pharmaceutical products have had wide press coverage here in Canada. In view of the large settlements made by the courts to people who have suffered harmful side effects from drugs, any pharmaceutical firm has an interest in knowing about all the effects of its products as quickly as possible. Attempting to hide the evidence of side effects would seem likely to increase, rather than reduce, a company's legal problems.

— The decreasing state financing of universities. There is no logical link between the idea of knowledge as a public good and the state financing of universities.

> Indeed, the notion of knowledge as the common property of humankind was around long before universities received funding from states. There is no problem if states contribute funds to universities, because universities can help nations to achieve certain goals. It is simply a question of proportion. Research on the benefits of higher education shows that the advantage to the individual graduate is larger than the benefit to society at large. It is reasonable, therefore, for people to pay part of the cost of their higher education. Some object that this will lower the participation rate of people from poorer backgrounds. However, the research, to which Canadian scholars have made an important contribution, shows clear results. In countries with free tuition in higher education the participation rate from people from disadvantaged backgrounds is less than in countries which combine tuition fees with a programme of grants and bursaries.

In basic education - primary and secondary - UNESCO policy, as well as World Bank policy, is opposed to direct or indirect tuition fees. This is not a contradiction. The economic, social and cultural benefits that society as a whole derives from basic education are very significant. This is why one of the objectives of the world campaign for education for all, which UNESCO coordinates, is:

> To ensure that by 2015 all children, especially girls, children in difficult circumstances, and from ethnic minorities have access to and complete free and compulsory primary education of good quality.

Myths about Education and Economic Growth. One of her conclusions is that we are wrong to promote universities by stressing primarily their contribution to economic growth. We should rather emphasise their role in the intellectual, cultural and social life of their country and the world. In this era of globalisation universities should promote international understanding. Since last year many people appeal to the 'clash of civilisations' as a way of understanding the current geopolitical tensions. Add to this post-modern attitudes and it is easy to exaggerate cultural differences and downplay the ideas of universal values and human rights. UNESCO, which like the rest of the United Nations system was founded on the Universal Declaration of Human Rights, viscerally opposes this new cultural relativism. One of our tools is the network of UNESCO chairs and the UNITWIN programme. This consists of five hundred professorial chairs in more than a hundred countries. They cover the range of UNESCO's interests and topics like human rights and press freedom.

Another feature of university development in this era of globalisation is the phenomenon of cross-border teaching. For students and scholars to be mobile is not, of course, new. Everyone knows about Erasmus, the 16 th century Dutch humanist who felt at home in all the universities of Europe. Even before that English students who were thrown out of the medieval University of Paris for bad behaviour helped to create Oxford University. Today courses are mobile as well as students. For instance, the UK Open University, my former institution, has some 30,000 students outside the UK. UNESCO is interested in cross-border teaching for three reasons.

First, we hope to persuade universities and countries not to make hasty judgements about this development, nor to confuse different phenomena. This form of teaching frequently uses distance education, which still arouses suspicion in some quarters, and often has a commercial flavour even - maybe especially - when the foreign institution is a public institution. Furthermore, it falls outside the control of national frameworks of higher education at a time when countries seem to want to control their universities more and more tightly. For these reasons UNESCO has just set up a Global Forum for Quality Assurance, Accreditation, and the Recognition of Diplomas in Higher Education. Its first meeting will take place in Paris in October. The key objective is simply to provide the opportunity for discussion between people bringing diverse perspectives from around the world.

In particular, and this is the second aspect of cross-border teaching that interests us, we want to know whether we should help to develop international instruments to help students and institutions make choices about courses and programmes from foreign sources. Ought we, for instance, to put together a guide to good practice, as was done in the 1970s in response to the controversies about correspondence education? Should we draw up a list of accrediting and quality assurance agencies that meet certain criteria of credibility and rigour? These are some of complex questions raised by the globalisation of higher education. Until now the accreditation of academic degrees and diplomas has been done almost exclusively at the national level.

The most significant exception is the International Baccalaureate. This diploma, covering the last two years of secondary education, today has very high credibility with universities throughout the world. It is governed and managed by an international non-governmental organisation. In passing that the programmes of the International Baccalaureate Organisation are in particularly widespread use here in Quebec. UNESCO is proud that it supported the creation of the International Baccalaureate Organisation thirty years ago and continues to enjoy close relations with it. The third aspect of cross-border teaching of particular interest to UNESCO relates to developing countries. These countries react to the phenomenon in different ways. For some it is an attack on national sovereignty. For others, cross-border education is a way of compensating for the lack of higher education capacity in the country caused by insufficient resources.

UNESCO wants to help countries in the second category while ensuring that the mobility of courseware does create yet another situation where globalisation causes money to flow from poor countries to rich ones promising development, namely the notion of open learning material. This is the equivalent, in the domain of teaching and learning of the open source software movement. The idea is simple. It is to make an institution's learning materials freely available on the web. It was the open universities that proposed this idea. In fact it came from a prestigious traditional university, the Massachusetts Institute of Technology.

The learning material that an institution can put on the web is only part of the process of university teaching and learning. It must be supported by a process of mediation between the student and the material through a tutor or teacher. Furthermore, there is always the need for a teacher to comment on the students' work and to assess their performance through tests and examinations. However, if the world's teachers can access a range of learning materials of quality and adapt them to their needs, they will be able to devote more time to supporting students and less to preparing to communicate basic content. Exchanging learning materials freely, knowledge can be refined and progressed in an open and collective way.

Open source learning materials are an encouraging example of the basic aim of UNESCO: full and equal opportunities for education for all, the unrestricted pursuit of objective truth, and the free exchange of ideas and knowledge. A form of scientific communism in the best academic tradition that will help the economic, cultural and social development of the whole world.

We can contribute to a strategy of sustainable human development if universities commit themselves to the notion of knowledge as a public good and make their learning materials freely available on the web. This global public good will help universities around the world, most notably those in developing countries, to improve their teaching while at the same time widening access to it and lowering the cost of higher education. It may seem like a revolutionary formula, but it is consistent with the best academic tradition.

Globalisation and National University Systems

Americans have clearly mastered the language of globalization. We now recognize that although we inhabit an immense continent bordered by two oceans, we cannot escape from the interconnectedness of the world. The "domestic" and the "foreign" have unclear lines of demarcation; the "other," for so long associated with peoples of other lands, is increasingly found among our own citizens, whose ethnic and cultural diversity expands every year. But in many respects, we seem to know the words but not the music.

Americans display a mass of contradictions in what they profess to value, and how we behave vis-à-vis our fellow citizens and the rest of the world. September 11 seems to have added to the national confusion. It drove home that globalised traffic runs two ways. The presence of the United States is felt in many ways in distant parts of the world, through trade, television and movies, and the Internet. And the world is present within the United States- in both benign and not so benign ways. September 11 brought home the fact that the United States, like other countries, is vulnerable. We discovered what the rest of the world has known for the long time-that we inhabit a dangerous planet. It underlined the reality that Americans know pitifully little about the rest of the world, and inspired some national soul-searching about that ignorance, especially in educational circles. And finally, September 11 posed the stark question: "How do others see us and why?" But the question of how the educational system prepares Americans for a global world did not arise out of nowhere on September 11. Those events put a quiet, much ignored conversation squarely on the table.

That conversation dates back to the Cold War. The launching of Sputnik spurred a substantial government investment in the development of area studies and language experts. Several government programs, including the Fulbright program, have remained to this day. Over the past 20 years, there have been a spate of national commissions, beginning with the 1979 President's Commission on Foreign Language and International Studies, which decried the absence of international and foreign language learning, and called for increased national and institutional investment in what we call "international education" in the United States.

Three opinion polls conducted by the American Council on Education suggest that the public recognizes the importance of international learning. The first poll, focusing on high school seniors, was conducted in 2000. Two broader polls were conducted in 2000 and then again 2002, measuring changes in public opinion after September 11.

We were surprised to see the high level of enthusiasm of high school seniors about international learning. Nearly 50 percent said they would like to study abroad. More than 70 percent considered it important that the institution they attend offer foreign language and international courses, study abroad programs, and opportunities to interact with foreign students. We also were surprised to see the high level of public support for international education-before and after September 11. In both the 2000 and 2002 surveys, more than 90 percent of respondents agreed that knowledge about international issues would be important to the careers of the younger generation.

About half said that such knowledge would be important for their own careers in the coming decade. Clearly, the public sees the future as getting more, not less, global in nature. In addition, the public sees such learning as a responsibility of colleges and universities, with 80 percent agreeing that higher education has a responsibility to provide education about international matters and 50 percent strongly agreeing.

The public is very supportive of foreign language learning and internationally focused courses. Eighty percent supported a high school foreign language requirement, both in 2000 and 2002. Those who strongly supported foreign language requirements grew from 23 percent to 51 percent, indicating that the intensity of support has increased. More than 70 percent in both polls supported a foreign language requirement in higher education. (While this may seem unremarkable to our European colleagues, remember, this is the United States.) Support for international education course requirements was unchanged from 2000 to 2002 at 77 percent.

The opinion data, even if they do inflate support because people may tell pollsters what they think they want to hear, are encouraging. But the gap between inclination and policy and practice is enormous. These generally favorable attitudes do not seem to translate into public policy, institutional action, or student behaviors. The rhetoric soars far above the reality, and closing this gap is an essential task for policy makers and institutional leaders. Let's look briefly at what is actually happening in terms of the three sectors-national government, U.S. colleges and universities, and students.

In May 2002, ACE and 35 higher education associations issued a call for "A Comprehensive National Policy on International Education" with a document of that name. We were careful to cast the call in terms that would resonate with members of Congress and other policy makers. We cited three national policy objectives:

1. Produce international experts and knowledge to address national strategic needs.
2. Strengthen U.S. ability to solve global problems.
3. Develop a globally competent citizenry and workforce.

The national spending on the major international education programs is roughly $300 million, less than one percent of federal discretionary expenditures for higher education. Even modest increases would be a great triumph given the current economic climate in the United States and the national obsession with defense and terrorism. It highly unlikely that the federal government will be a major player in helping institutions move forward on their international agendas. The interests of the government in promoting trade in education, which is an entirely different matter.

On the institutional front, we see a mixed picture. ACE has recently conducted three national surveys to understand what is happening on college and university campuses with respect to international education. The first survey yielded data from 732 institutions of all types about their policies and practices. The two others sampled 1,000 students and an equal number of faculty from these 732 institutions, querying them about their experiences and attitudes. On the institutional front, we found more rhetoric than action.

Some 35 percent of all institutions mention global or international learning in their mission statements. Fewer than three in 10 include it as one of the top five priorities in their strategic plan, and about a third have formally assessed the impact or progress of internationalization in the past five years. Yet more than half highlight opportunities for international education in their recruiting materials! Further signs of the relative unimportance of international education are the following facts: Only 5 percent of institutions consider international activity among their criteria for promotion and tenure. About four in 10 institutions require one or more courses with an international focus (generally as part of the general education requirement), and of those who do, 60 percent require only one course.

Perhaps the most dispiriting news is the choices that students themselves make. As you may know, in the U.S. system, students have approximately two years of general education, comprising an array of liberal arts courses that are foundational in nature. While a majority of students who go to four-year institutions in the United States have taken foreign languages in high school, few continue in college without a requirement to do so, and when they are compelled, most students end up starting all over again at the first level.

Language enrollments declined from a high of 16 percent of total enrollments in 1965 to less than 8 percent in the mid-1970s to the present. And we know that very few students achieve any usable level of language competency. The study abroad figures provide a striking discrepancy between what students imagine they might do, and what they actually do. Three percent actually study abroad before they graduate, compared with 50 percent of high school seniors who say they would like to do so.

These data suggest that if the United States is to provide an education that prepares its students to participate as workers and citizens of the world, then we have a huge challenge ahead. Our polling data also revealed that three in 10 respondents did not believe that their education prepared them to understand the complexities of world events, and nearly one in five college graduates felt ill-prepared. The burden is clearly on the educational system to make international learning an academic priority. We all know the obstacles to change in higher education. The capacity of U.S. colleges and universities to advance on internationalization. An increasing number of institutions are taking internationalization seriously. They are grappling with the challenges of infusing international courses and perspectives in the curriculum (where most U.S. students will learn about the world), and others are making efforts to boost the numbers of students studying abroad. We repeat the institutional survey in five years, we will see considerable progress-students today are more worldly, more curious about the world, more likely to have traveled and to see how closely our future is entwined with that of other peoples and nations.

We also have a new generation of faculty members coming into our classrooms, who grew up with technology and who we hope will be open to all kinds of changes. And, while there will ever be a huge national outcry for improved internationalization of higher education, employers and businesses do see its value. Over time, U.S. institutions have displayed a very healthy capacity for change and adaptation to the external environment. Only time will tell whether the environment is sufficiently propitious and the leadership sufficiently committed to turn the promise of internationalization into a reality.

American institutions have not been immune to seeing international education as a source of revenue. The more than 500,000 students from other countries who are currently in theUnited States are important sources of tuition dollars and fill places in graduate programs where there is a scarcity of Americans-in such fields as science and engineering. Some traditional (that is, nonprofit) universities have sought to expand their reach through distance learning and, in a few cases, off-shore campuses.

Many are finding that such ventures are time-consuming, expensive, and distracting, with uncertain returns. While the dot.com bubble has burst, and distance learning is turning out not to be a gold mine, some for-profit institutions, a fast-growing segment of U.S. higher education, seem to be having different experiences. The University of Phoenix's non-U.S. programs are growing rapidly, and other for-profits are eagerly eyeing the student market outside the United States.

The U.S. government, through the Office of the Trade Representative, has taken up the cause of selling U.S. higher education abroad. Since the nonprofits are not clamoring for this, we can surmise that the for-profit institutions and educational service providers such as testing agencies are eager to remove any barriers that will restrict their trade. We at the American Council on Education, and our partners in Canada and Europe, co-signed a declaration opposing GATS.

The trade negotiations are progressing, however, and while we have been unable to get education off the GATS table, we have been heard by our own trade delegation, and by our colleagues in higher education in other countries. Traditional colleges and universities have little to gain from GATS, and the potential costs seem to far outweigh the benefits. International exchanges and collaboration would not benefit from GATS and the ambiguities of the GATS language leave a lot of room for confusion and disputes.

We are well aware of the potential costs to developing countries; we have no illusions that that such trade is chiefly about access. Disadvantaged students are served by low-cost (and high-quality) education that is normally provided by national systems that are subsidized by governments. We see very little gain and much risk for our member institutions at the American Council on Education, and we know that developing countries are wary of the exporting powerhouses and the potential weakening of their national systems.

We must ensure that our graduates understand global environmental issues, that they know something about the history and cultures of faraway places (which are now part of the mosaic of U.S. life), and that they internalize the fact that not every human being on this planet speaks (or wants to speak) English. Our commitment to bringing in international students from other countries must remain strong because they have the potential to make a powerful contribution to the learning environment on U.S. campuses.

Right now, the confusion and delay in implementing a new federal system to keep track of international students is creating significant problems for institutions. If we remain unlikely to send our students into the world, then it is imperative that we bring the world to our campuses, through international students and technology. U.S. higher education has a lot to offer other nations, but we chronically underestimate what we have to gain from them. Joining the world is a vital agenda for the U.S. educational system and for its citizens.

5

Globalisation and Higher Education Challenges

The General Agreement on Trades in Service (GATS), plus other regional trade agreements, are testimony to the increased emphasis on trade and the market economy in this era of globalization. GATS is the first legal trade agreement which focuses exclusively on trade of services - as opposed to trade of products. It is administered by the World Trade Organization, a powerful organization with 144 member countries.

Education is one of the 12 service sectors covered by GATS. The purpose of GATS is to progressively and systematically promote freer trade in services by removing many of the existing barriers to trade. What does this mean for higher education? The current debate on the impact of GATS on higher education is divided, if not polarized. Critics focus on the threat to the role of government, the 'public good' and the quality of education. Supporters highlight the benefits that more trade can bring in terms of innovations through new providers and delivery modes, greater student access and increased economic gain. Trade liberalization has the potential to profoundly change the nature and provision of higher education provision and the role that government plays in that provision. The purpose of this chapter is to discuss both risks and opportunities that GATS brings to higher education and to identify some of the policy implications and issues which need further analysis.

Changes and Challenges in the Provision of Higher Education

The promotion of trade in education services is directly linked to a number of significant trends in higher education. These include

i) the emergence of new for- profit education providers,

ii) the growth of alternate electronic delivery modes both domestically and internationally,

iii) the response to the labour market,

iv) the increase in international academic mobility of students, professors and programs, and

v) the limited budget capacity (or political will) of government to meet the increasing domestic demand for higher education.

These trends are contributing to, as well as responding to, the expanding business of cross border delivery of higher education services. The GATS aims to capitalize on this market potential and promote further international trade in education services by establishing rules and procedures to eliminate barriers to trade.

The scenario of higher education provision is changing as providers - public and private, new and traditional - are delivering education services across national borders to meet the need in other countries. As a result, an exciting but rather complex, picture of higher education provision is emerging. So what? It is important to ask 'so what'. Many educators would point out that demand for higher education has been steadily increasing for years and that academic mobility for students, scholars, teachers and knowledge has been an integral aspect of higher education for centuries. This is true. But the picture is changing. Now, not only are more people moving; academic programs and providers are also moving across borders.

More and more, economic rationales and benefits are driving a large part of the international or cross border supply of education. This profit motive is a reality today, and applies to both private providers and in some cases public institutions. In short, the business or commercial side of education is growing. A recent OECD study estimated that the value of trade in education services was about $US 30 billion in 1999.

In fact, because this figure only includes students studying abroad and does not include other types of cross border education, it represents only a portion of the current level of trade. The future market is growing and this is one reason why education is one of the major sectors targeted by GATS. It is therefore important that educators are cognizant of the impact of trade liberalization on higher education and are taking steps to maximize the benefits and opportunities, and at the same time, minimize the threats to a robust and quality higher education system.

Purpose of GATS

The GATS is the first ever set of multilateral rules covering international trade in services. The GATS has three parts. The first part is the framework which contains the general principles and rules. The second part consists of the national schedules which list a country's specific commitments on access to their domestic market by foreign providers. The third part consists of annexes which detail specific limitations for each sector and are attached to the schedule of commitments. To understand GATS, it is essential to understand what kind of education services will be covered by GATS and what is meant by higher education services The GATS defines four ways in which a service can be traded, known as 'modes of supply'. These four modes of trade apply to all service sectors in GATS.

Trade in education is organized into five categories of service according to the UN Provisional Central Classification. They are Primary, Secondary , Higher, Adult and Other. The last three are of particular interest to this chapter. Clarification is needed to determine what is included each group, especially the 'Other' services group. At this time it is wide open and includes services as diverse as language testing, student recruitment and quality assessment of programs.

Major Principles

The overall framework contains a number of general obligations applicable to all trade in services regardless of whether a country has made a specific commitment to sectors or not. These are called unconditional obligations. There are three which are fundamental to this discussion.

The Most Favoured Nation (MFN) rule requires equal and consistent treatment of all foreign trading partners. It means treating one's trading partners equally. Under GATS, if a country allows foreign competition in a sector, equal opportunities in that sector should be given to service providers from all WTO members. This also applies to mutual exclusion treatment. For instance, if a foreign provider establishes branch campus in Country A, then Country A must permit all WTO members the same opportunity/ treatment. Or if Country A chooses to exclude Country B from providing a specific service, then all WTO members are excluded. It may apply even if the country has made no specific commitment to provide foreign access to their markets.

Therefore, MFN has implications for those countries who already are engaged in trade in educational services and/or who provide access to foreign education providers MFN is not the same as National Treatment which requires equal treatment for foreign providers and domestic providers. Once a foreign supplier has been allowed to supply a service in one's country there should be no discrimination in treatment between the foreign and domestic providers. It is important to note that it only applies where a country has made a specific commitment and exemptions are allowed. It is the national treatment principle which GATS critics believe can put education as a 'public good' at risk.

The third important element is Market Access. It means the degree to which market access is granted to foreign providers in specified sectors. Each country determines limitations on market access for each committed sector and lists in its national schedules those services for which it wishes to provide access to foreign providers. In addition to choosing which service sector/s will be committed, each country determines the extent of commitment by specifying the level of market access and the degree of national treatment they are prepared to guarantee.

The GATS is described as a voluntary agreement because countries can decide which sectors they will agree to cover under GATS rules. This is done through the preparation of their national schedules of commitments and through the 'request-offer' negotiation rounds. However, there are aspects of the agreement that question its voluntary nature, notably the built-in progressive liberalization agenda.

There are several aspects of GATS which are most controversial and require the serious attention of the higher education sector. According to the WTO, the agreement is deemed to apply to all measures affecting services except 'those services supplied in the exercise of governmental authority'. GATS supporters maintain that education provided and funded by the government is therefore exempted. The agreement states that in the exercise of governmental authority' means the service is provided on a 'non-commercial basis' and 'not in competition' with other service suppliers. These are the core issues at the heart of much of the debate about which services are covered. Education critics of the GATS maintain that due to the wide-open interpretation of 'non-commercial' and 'not in competition' terms, the public sector/government service providers may not in fact be exempt.

The situation is especially complicated in those countries where there is a mixed public/private higher education system; or where a significant amount of funding for public institutions is in fact, coming from the private sector; or where so called public institutions are providing privatized programs.

Another complication is that a public education institution in an exporting country is often defined as private/commercial when it crosses the border and delivers in the importing country. Therefore, one needs to question what 'non-commercial' really means in terms of higher education trade..

The debate about what 'not in competition' means is fuelled by the fact that there does not appear to be any qualifications or limits on the term.. For instance, if non-government providers (private non-profit or commercial) are delivering services, are they deemed to be in competition with government providers. In this scenario, public providers may be defined as being in competition by the mere existence of non-governmental providers. Does the method of delivery influence or limit the concept of in competition? Does the term cover situations where there is a similar mode of delivery, or for instance, does this term mean that public providers using traditional face-to-face classroom methods could be seen to be competing with foreign for-profit e-learning providers? These are unanswered questions which need clarification. Supporters of the GATS emphasize that education is to a large extent a government function and that the agreement does not seek to displace the public education systems and the right of government to regulate and meet domestic policy objectives. Critics express concern that the whole question of the protection of public services is very uncertain and potentially at risk by the narrow interpretation of what governmental authority means and a wide-open interpretation of what 'not in competition' and ' non- commercial basis' mean. Clearly, the question -which higher and adult education 'services exercised in governmental authority' are exempted from GATS - needs to be front and centre in the debate on the risks and opportunities associated with the agreement. Further and immediate action is required to gain clarification of which higher education providers or services are exempt from GATS.

The higher education sector is not the only sector who has been troubled by the ambiguity of the Clause 1.3. For instance the Financial Services sector, took an important step and prepared two annexes to the agreement which spelled how what was meant by financial services and secondly, delineated which ones were considered to be 'those services supplied in the exercise of governmental authority'. This is a constructive and concrete step that the higher education, or perhaps the entire education sector needs to consider.

Extent of country commitments

The education sector is one of the least committed sectors. The reason is not clear, but perhaps it can be attributed to the need for countries to strike a balance between pursuing domestic education priorities and exploring ways in which trade in education services can be further liberalized. Or it could be linked to the fact that to date, education has taken a very low priority in the major bilateral/regional trade agreements and rightly or wrongly, the same may be true for GATS.

Only 44 of the 144 WTO Members have made commitments to education, and only 21 of these have included commitments to higher education.The full unconditional commitments in higher education, perhaps with the interest and intent of encouraging foreign providers to help develop their educational systems. Australia's commitment for higher education covers provision of private tertiary education services including at the university level.

The European Union has included high education in their schedule with some limitations on all modes of trade except 'consumption abroad' which generally means foreign tuition paying students. As of March 2002, only four (USA, New Zealand, Australia, Japan) of the 21 countries with higher education commitments have submitted a negotiating proposal outlining their interests and issues. In June, 2002 all requests for liberalization of trade were due. The response to these requests, known as offers, are due in January of 2003.

This is a critical time for educators to be in close contact with the government education and trade officials to ensure that their opinions and expertise are heard. Different rationales and approaches exist. For example, a consumer oriented rationale can be interpreted as the need to provide a wider range of opportunities to consumers or the need to protect consumers by assuring appropriate levels of access to and quality of education services. The economic rationale can be understood as a way to increase trade revenues for exporting countries or it can be seen as a means to attract additional investment for education for importing countries. Other see the economic rationale as sabotaging the social development goals of education or even the scientific and knowledge purposes. Any number of issues can be used to illustrate the dichotomy of opinions on the rationales and benefits of increased trade in education. Different opinions exist between and within countries, and certainly among education groups as well. Further debate and analysis is necessary so that an informed position is taken on why or why not trade liberalization is attractive to an individual country and how trade agreements help or hinder achieving national goals and global interests.

The voices of developing countries need to be heard so that the benefits and risks associated with increased trade are clear and do not undermine their own efforts to develop and enhance their domestic higher education system. However, the voices and interests of the developing countries differ.

The opportunity to have foreign suppliers provide increased access to higher and adult education programs, or to invest in the infrastructure for education provision is attractive to some. The threat of foreign dominance or exploitation of a national system and culture is expressed by others. Trade liberalization 'for whose benefit' or 'at what cost' are key questions. Quality and accreditation are at the heart of this debate. The importance of frameworks for licensing, accreditation, qualification recognition and quality assurance are important for all countries whether they are importing and exporting education services.

Developing countries have expressed concern about their capacity to have such frameworks in place in light of the push toward trade liberalization and increased cross border delivery of education. The GATS, is one of many factors or instruments, which is encouraging greater mobility of professions. Although the agreement focuses on temporary movement of the labour force, it may lead to and facilitate permanent migration as well. The implications from increased mobility of teachers and researchers are particularly relevant to developing countries. It will be a major challenge to improve education systems if well-qualified professionals and graduates are being attracted to positions in other countries.

The impact of GATS on developing countries is the fundamental issue of their capacity to participate effectively in the global trading system and to be equal members in the WTO. Strong sentiments exist about the potential for trade rules to make poor countries poorer, instead of narrowing the gap between developed and developing countries. The perceived injustice regarding the expectation that poor nations are expected to remove trade barriers while rich nations retain barriers on certain goods, .contributes to the strong reactions of some developing countries about GATS in general.

Trade liberalization and trends in higher education

Trade liberalization is firmly enmeshed with other issues and trends in higher education and it is therefore challenging to isolate implications emanating from trade alone. These trends include:

1) the use of information and communication technologies (ICTS) for domestic and cross border delivery of programs;
2) the growing number of private for-profit entities providing higher education opportunities domestically and internationally;
3) the increasing costs and tuition fees faced by students of public (and private) institutions;

4) the need for public institution to seek alternate sources of funding which sometimes means engaging in for-profit activities or seeking private sector sources of financial support; and

5) the ability (or inability) of government to fund the increasing demand for higher and adult education The following sections identify questions and issues which need to be explored in terms of the impact of trade liberalization and GATS on policy directions for higher education.

Government and public education institutions have keenly felt the responsibility of ensuring access to education. In many, if not in most countries, this is a challenging issue as the demand for higher and adult education is steadily growing, often beyond the capacity of the country to provide it. This is one reason why some students are interested in out- of -country education opportunities and more providers are prepared to offer higher education services across borders. When increased trade liberalization is factored into this scenario the question of access becomes complicated.

Advocates of freer trade maintain that consumers/ students can have greater access to a wider range of education opportunities at home and abroad. Non-supporters of trade believe that access may be more limited because trade will commercialize education and consequently escalate the cost of education and perhaps lead to a two tiered system. This raises a fundamental question regarding the capacity and role of government with respect to providing open or limited access to higher education and the question of funding.

Many governments have limited budget capacity or at least lack the political will to allocate funds to meet the escalating costs of higher education. Can international trade provide alternate funding sources through new providers? Advocates of trade in education services would answer yes. Or, does it mean that public funding will be spread across a broader set of domestic and foreign providers because of GATS' rules such as national treatment and the unanswered question of whether public funding is seen as an unfair subsidy. Furthermore, does the presence of foreign providers signal to government that they can decrease public funding for higher education thereby jeopardizing domestic publically funded institutions. Does international trade in education advantage some countries, such as those with well-developed capacity for export, and disadvantage others in terms of funding or access?

The development of a regulatory framework to deal with the diversity of providers and new cross border delivery modes becomes more critical as international trade increases. In some countries, this will likely mean a broader approach to policy which involves licensing, regulating, monitoring, both private (profit and non-profit) and foreign providers in order to ensure that national policy objectives are met and public interests protected. More work is necessary to determine how domestic/ national regulatory frameworks are compatible with, or part of a larger international framework and how they relate to trade agreement rules.

New types of education providers, new delivery modes, new cross border education initiatives, new levels of student mobility, new opportunities for trade in higher education- all this can spell further confusion for the recognition of qualifications and transfer of academic credits. This is not a new issue. Trade agreements are not responsible for the creation of this confusion, but they contribute to making it more complicated and also to making resolution more urgent.

National and international recognition of qualifications and the transfer of credits have already been the subject of a substantial amount of work and the UNESCO Global Forum on International Quality Assurance, Accreditation and the Recognition of Qualifications is currently focussing on this important issue.

Increased transnational education activity and new legal trade rules require that more attention be given to the question of quality assurance and accreditation of cross border education programs and providers. It is clear that national quality assurance schemes are being challenged by the complexities of the international education environment. Not only is it important to have domestic/national policy and mechanisms, it is equally important that attention be given to developing an international policy approach to quality assurance and accreditation.

Can coherence between a domestic/national system and an international policy framework actually strengthen national quality schemes not weaken them? Clearly there are risks and opportunities associated with this issue but doing nothing is a risk unto itself. Quality assurance of higher education is in some countries regulated by the sector, and in others by the government to a greater or lesser degree. The key point is that authority for quality assurance, regulation, accreditation for cross border delivery needs to be examined and guided by stakeholders and bodies related to the education sector and not left in the hands of trade officials or the market.

Mobility of professionals

GATS is facilitating the mobility of professionals to meet the high demand for skilled workers. This impacts many of the service sectors and has particular implications for the mobility of teachers and scholars in the higher education sector. In many countries, the increasing shortage of teachers is resulting in active recruitment campaigns across borders. Since many teachers and researchers want to move to countries with more favourable working conditions and salaries, there is a real concern that the most developed countries will benefit from this mobility of education workers.

Culture and acculturation

Last, but certainly not least, is the issue of culture. Education is a process through which cultural assimilation takes place. Concern about the homogenization of culture, through cross border supply of education is expressed by GATS sceptics. Advocates maintain, that a new hybridization and fusion of culture will evolve through increasing mobility and the influence of ICTs. In fact, they believe that this has been happening for decades and is a positive development. Once again, the divergence of opinion shows that there are new opportunities and new threats to consider, especially on the question of acculturation.

Trade dominates

Finally, it needs to be asked whether trade liberalization has the potential of dominating the higher education agenda? There is a risk of 'trade creep' where education policy issues are being increasingly framed in terms of trade and economic benefit. Even though, domestic challenges in education provision are currently front and centre on the radar screen of most countries, the issue of international trade in education services will likely increase in importance and perhaps at the expense of other key objectives and rationales for higher education such as social, cultural and scientific development and the role of education in promoting democracy and citizenship.

There seem to be more questions than answers about the impact of GATS and trade liberalization. The questions are complex as they deal with technical/legal issues of the agreement itself; education policy issues such as funding, access, accreditation, quality and intellectual property and; the larger more political/moral issues for society such as the role and purpose of higher education and the 'public good' or 'market commodity ' approach to education. GATS is new, complex, untested and a work-in-progress. It is therefore difficult to understand or predict its impact. The one thing that is certain though, is that the higher education sector needs to be better informed and more involved in the debate and provide advice to the trade officials about potential unintended consequences or possible opportunities.

At this stage, it appears that there are more questions than clear answers about the impact and implications of GATS on higher education. The questions are both complex and contentious. They deal with technical/legal issues of the agreement itself; education policy issues such as funding, access, accreditation, quality and intellectual property and, the larger more political/moral issues for society such as the role and purpose of higher education and whether education is a 'public good' and/or 'tradeable commodity.

This chapter ends with the recommendation that education policy makers, researchers and senior administrators give more attention to analysing the opportunities, risks and policy implications emanating from the inclusion of higher education services in GATS and other international trade agreements. The education sector needs to work more closely with the trade officials, negotiators and researchers to become better informed of the issues but also to exchange information and provide advice on the implications for education policy and influence future directions of trade of higher education services.

Trade officials also need to take the initiative to consult with educators. It is suggested that international governmental bodies and non-governmental organizations as well as regional and national education groups give more priority to the policy issues emanating from trade liberalization and be proactive in examining how to fully benefit from new opportunities that are available from global competitive trade and be mindful of risks and unintended consequences. Finally, it is important not to overstate the impact of GATS. Trade in education was alive and well prior to trade agreements. It will undoubtedly increase under the auspices of GATS but the policy issues such as funding, access and quality assurance need to be addressed and managed by the education sector and not left to the purview of trade agreements and the WTO.

New Models for Higher Education

We are witnesses to a unique era of human history

during which global forces are combining to produce rapid and profound change on a heretofore unknown scale. A sense of disequilibrium pervades every aspect of our lives and is placing great stress on society's fundamental institutions. None of our systems are spared, including our global system of higher education. Academicians face a unique dilemma. By profession, we study the changes and forces for change in society and its institutions. We measure, evaluate, and predict these changes and their ramifications to other areas of life and culture. We propose interventions that will deal with the dislocations and chaos our organizations face. Ironically, many of us seem to believe that our own educational institutions and networks of institutions should remain static-as if that were even a possibility; as if there were a platonic form for colleges and universities to which we should be attempting to conform. Like it or not, of course, higher education is as subject to the aforementioned forces as any other societal entity.

As with every other type of institution, we know that new structural forms will appear as well in higher education-the result of varied combinations of economic, demographic, cultural, and technological forces. Some of these will disappear as quickly as they arose. Others, having met some basic societal need, will survive and even displace revered but obsolete structures that have been unable to adapt. This is not to suggest that traditional colleges and universities will disappear. It is most likely that a variety of institutional types will exist and prosper. But some will fail and all will invariably be changed by these forces. This chapter describes one institutional variation, the University of Phoenix, which arose in the United States over the last quarter century-the result of the forces adumbrated above.

In 1976, the leading edge members of the Baby Boom generation were just turning 30. That same year saw the introduction of the first personal computer, the Apple I—an event that signaled the birth of a new economic system through which intellectual capital would eventually supplant industrial might as the dominant global economic force. These milestones also marked the beginning of a sea change in American higher education, though many (perhaps even most) within that system did not recognize it at the time. Considered together, these phenomena suggested that the jobs that would make up the workforce of the future were only just beginning to be created or imagined.

In order to fill those jobs, the bulk of the new workforce would require different, higher-level knowledge and skills than those needed in a manufacturing economy. At the same time, the largest-ever age cohort of the population, working adults, would be going through the stages of life during which they would be most affected by the coming economic dislocation and would need advanced education to adapt to these changes. It was in this historical context in 1976, that Dr. John Sperling, a Cambridge-educated economist and professor-turned-entrepreneur, founded University of Phoenix. Sperling anticipated the confluence of technological, economic, and demographic forces that would in a very short time herald the return of ever-larger numbers of working adults to formal higher education. Over the course of the past quarter-century, University of Phoenix has become the largest private university in the U.S., with a current enrollment of nearly 140,000. It operates campus locations where face-to-face instruction is provided, in 26 states, Puerto Rico, British Columbia, and Rotterdam in the Netherlands. It also currently enrolls nearly 50,000 degree in its Online Campus, including representatives from 40 different countries.

The University attributes its growth to an unwavering focus on serving its unique student population, including the creation of a teaching/learning model designed specifically for working adults. It has been equally devoted to creating an organizational culture in which innovation and continuous improvement are core values. The University's future includes plans for international expansion, primarily through its Online Campus. Many of these same dynamics seen in the United States are also evident in other areas of the world. Increasingly, global economic development will depend not only on educating young people to take their places as citizens and preparing them to earn living wages, but also on the revitalization of the existing population of working adults through the practices of lifelong learning. Responding to global economic competition will require a more rapid retooling of a country's work force than waiting for new workers to enter will allow. Thus, institutions like University of Phoenix may offer lessons about structuring higher education for non-traditional students.

The focus of the research was to explore teaching/ learning systems for the delivery of educational programs and services to working adult students who wished to complete or further their education in ways that complemented both their experience and current professional responsibilities. At that time colleges and universities were organized primarily around serving the needs of the 18-22 year-old undergraduate student. That is not at all surprising, given that the large majority of those enrolled were residential students of traditional college age, just out of high school. According to Sperling working adult students were invisible on the traditional campus and were treated as second-class citizens:

> Other than holding classes at night (and many universities did not even do this), no efforts were made to accommodate their needs. No university offices or bookstores were open at night. Students had to leave work during the day to enroll, register for classes, buy books or consult with their instructors and advisors. Classes were held two or three nights per week and parking was at the periphery of a large campus. The consequence, according to Dr. Sperling was that most working adult students were unable to finish a four-year program in less than eight years, or a two-year program in less than four years.

Sperling's research convinced him not only that working adult students were interested in furthering their educational goals but also that they differed from their younger counterparts in significant ways. He saw a growing need for institutions sensitive to and designed around the learning characteristics and life situations of the working adult population. He suggested how these institutions would pioneer new approaches to curricular and program design, teaching methods, and student services. These beliefs eventually resulted in the creation of University of Phoenix, and they continue to this day to inspire the University's mission, purposes, and strategies. As an institution, University of Phoenix is unique in its single-minded commitment to the educational needs of working adults. This focus informs the University's teaching and learning model, approach to designing and providing student services, and academic and administrative structure. It also guides the institution as it plans and prepares to meet the needs of working adult students.

The University's Statement of Mission and Purposes focuses clearly on student learning and identifies that focus as the vehicle though which broader institutional goals will be pursued. It also emphasizes innovation, convenience, continuous improvement, and service quality as essential to the achievement of the University's mission.

The mission of University of Phoenix is to educate working adults to develop the knowledge and skills that will enable them to achieve their professional goals, improve the productivity of their organizations, and provide leadership and service to their communities.

— To facilitate cognitive and affective student learning-knowledge, skills, and values-and to promote use of that knowledge in the student's work place.

— To develop competence in communication, critical thinking, collaboration, and information utilization, together with a commitment to lifelong learning for enhancement of students' opportunities for career success.

— To provide instruction that bridges the gap between theory and practice through faculty members who bring to their classrooms not only advanced academic preparation, but also the skills that come from the current practice of their professions.

— To use technology to create effective modes and means of instruction that expand access to learning resources and that enhance collaboration and communication for improved student learning.

— To assess student learning and use assessment data to improve the teaching/learning system, curriculum, instruction, learning resources, counseling and student services.

— To be organized as a for-profit institution in order to foster a spirit of innovation that focuses on providing academic quality, service, excellence, and convenience to the working adult.

— To generate the financial resources necessary to support the university's mission.

A Teaching/Learning Model

Because University of Phoenix exists to serve the working adult population, the University's teaching/learning model is grounded in the theoretical and empirical literature of adult learning and cognitive psychology, and employs best practice from the adult education literature. Its essential features include:

Active learning

The learner's active involvement in the learning process is essential to good practice. Creating instruction that utilizes the affective domain enables the adult learner to connect more extensively with the cognitive domain. Thus, University of Phoenix classrooms are intended to be dynamic learning spaces. Instructors are expected to serve as facilitators of learning who manage the learning process by engaging learners in a variety of activities (lectures being but one) that lead students to an understanding of course content and the development of academic and professional competence. By involving students in a variety of learning activities, respect is demonstrated for diverse ways of learning and knowing. Interaction and participation in classes and learning teams is expected. While there are certainly didactic elements in every course, these are augmented and enhanced by student participation through discussion, debate, reflection, and application.

A learning environment based on collaboration

The effectiveness of cooperation and collaboration in enhancing learning is well and widely documented. Structures that encourage and facilitate collaboration are central to the teaching/learning model. Working adults generally come to formal learning activities with significantly greater life and work experience than their younger counterparts. This means that learners themselves can be invaluable resources in enhancing their own and others' learning. Traditional pedagogy emphasizes a top-down, vertical transfer of information. Adult students with rich and varied experience find benefit in instructional practices that encourage collaboration. This adds a robust "horizontal" dimension to the learning exchange as adult students teach and learn from one another.

A unique program format

University of Phoenix does not operate according to a traditional academic calendar. New student cohorts can begin at any time and classes are held throughout the year without traditional quarter or semester breaks. Typically, graduate courses at University of Phoenix meet for six consecutive weeks and undergraduate courses meet for five weeks. When a course ends, the next course usually begins the following week. This intensive calendar allows adult students to achieve their educational goals in a more time-efficient manner. The

University's low student/faculty ratio and class sizes that average 13 students facilitate active learning and collaboration, encourage time-on-task, and foster high student-faculty interaction. As a rule, students take only one course at a time. This allows focus on one subject. This structure enhances learning and helps students balance ongoing professional and personal responsibilities.

On-campus instruction

During a typical on-campus course, students participate in two instructional activities each week-a four-hour workshop facilitated by the faculty member-and a 4-5 hour learning team session. Learning teams are intact groups of from three to five students drawn from within the larger cohort. Learning Teams foster students' abilities to collaborate-a competency expected of employees in information age organizations and one of the University's primary learning goals. Faculty members closely monitor the learning team activities, outcomes and processes through review of learning team logs and charters.

Online Campus Instruction

Students who complete their academic programs through the Online Campus participate in an asynchronous electronic conferencing format that allows them to participate at the times and places that work best for them within required timeframes. The University is also developing a new instructional format called FlexNet-a hybrid delivery method that blends the campus and online modalities.

An emphasis on application and relevance

There is wide agreement in the literature that adults learn best when bridges are built between new knowledge and the learner's experience. Practices that encourage reflection and application are based on the recognition that a learner's experience provides a context through which he or she is more able to construct meaning from new information. It also makes learning relevant to the learners, increasing affective connection with subject matter and the likelihood that they will respond with a deep versus surface approach to learning. In University of Phoenix courses, students' past experiences and current circumstances are interwoven with subject matter in class discussions as well as in individual and learning team assignments. Students very often say they are able to apply at work the next day what they learned in class the night before.

Building professional competence

The University's faculty leadership has established five broad "learning goals" that guide curriculum development, instruction, learning assessment, and program evaluation and improvement. The first of these goals, Professional Competence and Values, relates to the discipline-specific course and program content. University of Phoenix wants its graduates to attain levels of theoretical and practical disciplinary knowledge appropriate to the levels of degrees or credentials they are earning (i.e., bachelor, master, or doctoral level). The remaining four goals relate to the development of competence in essential intellectual and social processes that will enable graduates to practice their professions successfully. They are Critical Thinking and Problem Solving, Communication, Information Utilization, and Collaboration.

Convenience of time and place

University of Phoenix classroom programs are offered at times and in places that are convenient to working adults. Classes are held primarily in the evening and on weekends when working adults are most likely to need access. Wherever possible, campuses and learning centers are locted at strategic locations near major freeways and thoroughfares that permit convenient access Campus facilities, including both instructional and administrative space, are generally housed in Class A or equivalent space, and are established under long-erm leases of from 5-10 years. This allows the institution to respond with flexibility t shifts in population.

Adult-friendly student Services

University of Phoenix has found that adult students tend to hold higher expectations of student services than teir younger counterparts. These students expect from the University the same levels of attention and convenience they expect from any other service provider. Increasingly, tis implies 24 x 7 access to student services. Services are provided through electronic or telephone access as much as possible though person-to-person service is always available. For example, rather than requiring students to drive to a campus bookstore, texts and course materials are ordered via the Internet or by toll-free telephone and delivered directly to the student's home.

Students attending University of Phoenix Online courses enjoy the same commitment to student service as campus students. Through years of experience in online education, the University has learned that an even greater investment in the quality and availability of student services must be made to ensure that students who attend courses at a distance persist and succeed. The Online Campus is structured around the particular needs and abilities of the kinds of students who select distributed learning as their preferred method.

University's Faculty

From the founding of University of Phoenix to the present day perhaps the greatest institutional challenge has been to build innovative structures that support the University's unique mission. The result is a model that assures that essential roles performed by the faculty in any teaching university are also fulfilled at University of Phoenix-though sometimes in a different fashion. To a degree, this model represents what has come to be referred to as an unbundled or disaggregated approach.

Based on his initial field-based research in the early 1970s the University's founder, Dr. John Sperling concluded that a classroom full of adults enrolled in professional education is a qualitatively distinct place from one filled with 18-22 year-olds. He found that adult students brought very different expectations regarding the kind of instruction they receive than did his younger students in a traditional setting. According to recent research by the College Board more than 80% of adults who return for advanced education do so because of a desire to advance in their professions and careers. That percentage is up from 70% just a decade ago. From an instructional standpoint, the most significant issue relates to the resulting expectation that instruction will be of immediate practical relevance.

This does not mean that working adults do not recognize a need for or desire an understanding of the theory of a discipline-especially when they come to understand how a grasp of theory helps them in situations and events in the professional setting and enables them to predict the consequences of interventions. They do expect, however, that the theory will be taught in the context of practice and application. As a result, they often display a lower degree of patience for instructors who are not equipped by experience to do this. This is significant because working adults, having consciously chosen to pursue education, often at significant personal and financial cost, are more likely to vote with their feet and pocketbooks. This should not be taken to indicate that adult students want their education to be easy-they readily grasp that rigor and credibility are related. It has been the University's experience that in order to attract and retain adult students; format and instruction must be consistent with their self-perceived needs as well as the educational needs an institution identifies for them.

John Sperling discovered that the faculty members favored by these students, and those from whom they learning more, brought to the classroom not only advanced academic preparation in a field but also the significant practical professional experience that facilitated the marriage of theory and practice. He also noted, based on his comparison of learning outcomes, that there was no degradation of results. He ultimately concluded that an institution whose sole mission was to serve working adults could craft an innovative model that used these insights to its advantage and set out to do so.

Implications of the Faculty Model: Outcomes data suggest that a teaching faculty comprised predominantly of professional practitioners is an effective way to educate working adults. Adopting this model has required, however, that University of Phoenix develop processes and support structures for ensuring that essential faculty roles are appropriately filled. The roles filled by the faculties of most higher education institutions generally include research, teaching-which refers to a group of activities that include classroom instruction, grading and evaluation, student advisement, participation in academic governance, and service to the larger community. Additionally, most colleges and universities rightly cede control of the content of the curriculum to the faculty. It is often implied, however, that each member of a faculty is responsible to shoulder all of these roles. Even if this were possible, the reality is that individual members tend to gravitate to those tasks and roles for which they have particular liking or expertise. This "unbundling" of faculty roles occurs naturally. Through identifying the academic process goals that various faculty roles have evolved to serve, University of Phoenix has disaggregated the process and assigned specialized responsibility for its parts.

The University employs a core cadre of full-time faculty members. These faculty members spend the majority of their time in teaching or instruction-related activities. They provide instructional leadership, oversee academic quality assurance, and provide guidance and support for the rest of the faculty. They are involved in faculty selection and training, participate in curricular oversight activities, and serve as members of the Academic Program Councils. This core cadre of full-time faculty assumes crucial leadership for the various academic processes and provides consistent oversight of the curricula and instructional quality. It may also be useful, however, to describe University philosophy regarding the part-time "practitioner" faculty. Significant dependence on these professionals to fulfill teaching and other governance roles at the University has made it essential that the University view them and support them differently than part-time faculty members are often viewed. For example, University of Phoenix purposely refrains from using the term "adjunct" because the University's faculty model requires that they not be positioned as adjunct to the full-time faculty. All faculty members, whether full-or part-time, are viewed as full and essential members of the University faculty community. The professional practitioners who serve on the faculty participate in the same assessment and developmental processes as their full-time colleagues.

Curricular Oversight

It is widely accepted that responsibility for the curriculum of an academic program properly rests with full-time members of a faculty who are both firmly grounded and current in the body of knowledge of that discipline. This guarantees the coherence of program structure and design as well as the appropriateness of requirements, objectives, and outcomes. Traditionally, this process is the province of Curriculum Committees to which faculty representatives are assigned. At University of Phoenix, the equivalent of the Curriculum Committee is the Academic Program Council. Academic Program Councils are created for each academic program within a college. These councils include at least four full-time faculty members and four practitioner faculty members recognized as instructional leaders and content specialists. Selected administrative specialists serve as staff advisors on operations and logistical issues.

In a traditional academic setting, individual faculty members are responsible for the design of their own course outlines and syllabi. It is assumed that the disciplinary grounding of full-time faculty members qualifies them to determine the objectives and content for a course based on the current body of knowledge. With a teaching faculty comprised largely of professional practitioners who are not full-time academicians, the University must ensure that course content reflects the current state of theoretical knowledge in a particular field. For this reason, teams selected from both full-time and practitioner members of the faculty are recruited and contracted to create an expanded syllabus or "module" for each University of Phoenix course. The teaching faculty member is then able to marry the sound theoretical foundation contained in the course module to the knowledge of current practice in the profession.

Curriculum development teams that create these modules are comprised of both full-time and practitioner faculty members collaborate with a curriculum development manager who oversees the documentation process, and an instructional designer who ensures that the course "maps" appropriately to program objectives and the University's Learning Goals.. Additionally, a set of teaching notes is created to assist the preparation of a faculty member assigned to teach the course.

Finally, the team identifies and describes the academic and professional qualifications a faculty member must have to be approved to teach the course. The course module is not set in stone, however. Latitude is given to the teaching faculty member to exercise academic judgment. He or she may choose to enhance or change assignments and design learning activities not included in the teaching notes. The basic requirement is that the course must be taught and assessed to the objectives identified by the faculty team at the appropriate academic level.

Teaching

The University practices a collaborative, facilitative instructional model. For this reason, and because the majority of University of Phoenix instructors are not traditional full-time faculty members for whom teaching is a primary occupation, it is incumbent on the University to ensure that those appointed to the faculty can demonstrate the ability or potential to teach effectively in this environment. To this end, all faculty candidates participate in a rigorous screening and assessment process. It begins with a resume or curriculum vitae review to ensure that they meet the basic requirements for approval, which include a graduate degree from a regionally accredited institution and at least five years of employment in their field-two of which must have occurred subsequent to completion of a master's degree. Practitioner faculty candidates must also be currently employed in the discipline in which they teach.

Content interview with an experienced faculty member from the candidate's discipline. The purpose is to ensure that candidates bring the breadth, depth, and current knowledge of the content area in which they will be teaching. Candidates are then invited to demonstrate their ability to facilitate learning in an assessment experience during which candidates are observed and evaluated by senior faculty members. Additionally, all new faculty members complete extensive training as part of the Faculty Certification Process-a four-session course augmented by Web-and paper-based readings and training modules.

This experience is designed to model appropriate facilitation practice at the University and provides additional content and training in areas such as adult learning theory and practice, facilitation skills, learning team administration, grading, evaluation, assessment, governance and administrative procedures, and the University Library. The Faculty Certification module was developed by a team of full-time faculty members from four of the seven regions across the University, two representatives from central administration academic affairs and an instructional design consultant Those who successfully complete this process then apply for approval to teach specific courses offered by the University. The Dean or his/her designee judge the member's academic and professional experience specific to the faculty course approval requirements created for the course. The final step for a new faculty member is participation in a mentorship with an experienced faculty member during the first course he or she teaches.

Ongoing training and development opportunities are made available to the entire faculty through regular faculty training meetings and Web-based training modules. Additionally, faculty members receive a

Faculty Handbook that includes the Faculty Standards with which faculty members are expected to comply in order to remain in good standing with the University, as well as all pertinent policies, procedures, and expectations.

Faculty scholarship

University of Phoenix is a teaching institution whose focus is professional education for working adults. While formal academic research is not a requirement of the practitioner faculty, the University recognizes that an important precursor to fulfillment of the fundamental aspects of our Mission and Purposes related to student learning and development is a faculty that engages appropriately in scholarly activities. In an institution that serves a specialized population and employs a disaggregated or unbundled faculty model, this necessitates a different approach to scholarship than would be found in a traditional setting. Contrary to perceptions that a faculty comprised so largely of practitioners would not actively engage the "scholarship of discovery", a recent compilation of scholarship activities of the University's faculty indicates otherwise.

The University has recently begun a process of automating its faculty files. This has allowed the aggregation of the academic and professional activities in which the University's faculty is involved and the scholarship produced. The initial results of the survey among full-time faculty suggest that there is significant ongoing scholarship-in all the dimensions described by Boyer-taking place within the Faculty. Additionally, the University's Virtual Community of Scholars, is an online community that fosters exchange of research ideas and resources among faculty and doctoral students.

Faculty chat rooms serve as links for exchange of best practices, both in education and in real world application and trends across disciplines. It is designed to promote scholarship and to provide a forum for the University's faculty to appropriately publish their research and learning. This new endeavor is still in the early stages of development.

Over the last two decades, University of Phoenix has made significant investments in developing and maintaining institutional research capabilities. These systems measure and evaluate the University's effectiveness in achieving objectives and improving institutional processes. The foundation of the University's evaluation and assessment efforts was laid in the 1980's. This foundation continues to rest on two pillars refined in the early 1990's-the Academic Quality Management System (AQMS) focusing on the performance of educational support systems including faculty, curriculum, and student services, and the Adult Learning Outcomes Assessment (ALOA) focusing on the measurement of student learning in both the cognitive and affective domains.

These assessment systems have brought significant public recognition to University of Phoenix over the past decade and the institution has continued innovation in this area through a "reengineering" of its assessment processes over the last two years.

When University of Phoenix enters a community, it is sometimes perceived as a threat to existing institutions. Initial concerns tend to subside with the realization that the University focuses on a different population segment than most others. Additionally, the resources spent to attract new students stimulate a general interest in higher education and, ultimately, contributes to an overall increase in adult students returning to other institutions as well. The University of Phoenix provides social and economic benefits by helping to meet the educational needs of working adults without adversely impacting the existing higher education system. As a for-profit, adult-centered institution, the University does not draw on states' educational resources, but instead offers economic advantages. Some of these advantages include:

a) withdrawal of less federal and state income taxes and local property and sales taxes, returning more to the public treasury than their students take out in the form of grants and below-market federally insured loans;

b) access to private capital for funds needed for start-up and/or expansion; and

c) operation from leased commercial space that can be designed and built in a matter of months to meet student needs. Perhaps, most importantly, the University contributes to state economies by providing educational opportunities so that working adults can enhance their knowledge and skills and as a result, continue to be productive citizens.

With the University's emphasis on professional programs, these are some of the areas where it is making a contribution in the communities it serves:

— Twenty-five percent of the University's enrollments during 2001 entered degree programs where significant national shortages are being (Information

Systems and Technology, Teacher Education, Health Sciences and Nursing, Counseling and Human Services).

- Since its establishment in 1976, 125,000 students have graduated from University of Phoenix. In the year 2000, more than 25,000 students graduated from University of Phoenix and continued to be a part of the nation's workforce.
- Nearly 65 percent of University of Phoenix students who begin two, three, or four-year degree programs, whether in campus-based or Online Campus programs, will complete them, despite the competing interests of work, family, and community. This is in contrast to a national graduation rate in the U.S. of 58 percent.
- University of Phoenix has demonstrated a significantly higher than average level of participation and graduation by members of minority populations. Fully 40% of University of Phoenix students identify themselves as members of an ethnic minority.
- 65 percent of the University's candidates for admission come from referrals from satisfied students, alumni and their employers.
- 94 percent of graduates said they would recommend the University of Phoenix to another adult student.
- 43 percent of graduates receiving a promotion since completing their degrees.

In the lives of its many adult students, the University's contributions will be life changing. The educational experience provided has helped foster new ways of seeing the world and has improved quality of life; it has contributed to the success of the organizations as they become more effective professionals, thinkers and problem-solvers; and it enables them to make contributions in their communities and to the larger society.

6

Education in Globalising World

Education is undergoing constant changes under the effects of globalisation. The introduction of information technology and communication is changing the delivery of education, changing the roles of students and teachers, and producing a shift in society from industrialisation towards an information-based society. The changes in education due to globalisation have also had profound effects upon a broad spectrum of cultures leading to suggestions of a new form of cultural imperialism. In addition, the structure of education is being altered to enable it to compete on an open, global market, leading to the 'commodification' of education. Educational institutions around the world are being forced to compete globally, by engaging in entrepreneurial activities to sustain themselves in an uncertain and competitive world. Globalisation impacts on many facets of life, including education. Rapid developments in technology and communication are foreseeing changes within school systems across the world as ideas, values and knowledge, vital to education, cross nation states and boundaries.

The rise of a global society, driven by technology and communication developments are shaping children, the future citizens of the world into 'global citizens', intelligent people with a broad range of skills and knowledge to apply to a competitive, information based society. The future of countries often lies within their ability to compete in a global market where industrial based economies are giving way to knowledge based industries, realising the importance of "knowledge, skills and the intellectual capacity to meet the challenges of accelerated change and uncertainty".

Education is becoming a lifelong learning and training process, developing transferable skills and knowledge that can be applied to competitive markets where knowledge and information is being traded as a commodity. Globalisation is also creating a fast paced, competitive environment through technology and communication which education systems must keep up with. "Children cannot be effective in tomorrow's world if they are trained in yesterdays skills" is a statement that is particularly true for citizens of western, developed societies which are rapidly embracing the advancing technological and communication development into education systems.

Countries are now realising the economic potential and value of technology in education "if we, as a nation, are to compete in the global market place in the decade to come we must become leading and proficient users of information technology". As such, it is vital that education systems embrace and implement technology into their schools to produce citizens capable of living in the twenty first century where technology is encroaching more and more into everyday life.

The introduction of technology into the classroom is changing the nature of delivering education to students from primary through to tertiary levels. Print literacy, although still widely used is gradually giving way to a new form of electronic literacy "more and more programs and education materials are becoming available in electronic form, more and more teachers are preparing materials in electronic form; and more and more students are generating papers, assignments and projects in electronic form". Blackboards are now being replaced by video projection screens, books with storage device servers and CD ROMs as well as the emergence of on-line digital libraries.

Even exams and grades are gradually becoming available through electronic means and notebooks are starting to give way to laptops. Also, students can be examined through computer managed learning systems and do tutorial exercises on a computer rather than in a classroom. Such developments in education portray that there has been a shift from industrialisation to information based societies. Subsequently, technology is foreseeing a change in the education environment towards a reliance on electronic sources to deliver material. With such changes and the emergence of video conferencing and the internet, the barriers of distance are being broken down at a rapid rate, a key aspect of globalisation.

Children and adults can now learn in a variety of ways and no longer have to be physically present at an education institution in order to learn, a definite advantage of flexible delivery systems. It allows for exploration of new areas of learning and thinking. It is estimated there are over 43 million hosts connected to the internet with access to approximately 320 million pages of information, figures that reflect the potential influence the internet can have on education alone. However, there is little doubt that the development and deployment of information and communication technologies will have enormous implications on access, institutional functioning and the teaching and learning process.

Many institutions as direct providers of learning opportunities to students are using technology to deliver its programs, courses and tuition support. In fact, the information technology revolution is also foreseeing the development of new kinds of institutions such as 'virtual universities' which are delocalised across cyberspace, institutions with no real buildings and location as such, just web pages providing access to information, knowledge and ideas.

The transformation of technology and communications into education systems is being seen as a dawn of an new era where most colleges and universities must decide whether to change a little and remain in the academic candle industry or change a lot and launch themselves into the academic electrical business. An increase in information technology businesses has been developing and replacing industrialisation since World War II. The rapid growth of television services, with their immense influence as media of mass communication, has been very relevant in the technological shift. Other large contributions to this shift include the transistor and space satellites.

The transistor is particularly significant for computers and control engineering whilst the establishment of space satellites has played a dramatic role in telephone and television communication.

However the primary advancement made in communication and information based technology over the years is the Internet, which is a massive network of computers located throughout the world. These computers maintain libraries of text, images, computer software, and other forms of data that can be accessed by anyone, anywhere, at any time. However, for this implementation of technology and communication to be successful and to educate a society, both the students and teachers need to be technologically literate. Thus the roles of the teachers and students are changing.

The introduction of the internet into classrooms means that students must filter through a mass of information that is available to them and learn to deal with the complexity of this information. The internet is providing students with an interconnected world of knowledge to explore which they must decipher for themselves. Communication technology is offering new challenges for students of all abilities as they can discuss issues of concern with their fellow students from around the world, thus developing communication and interpersonal skills, fostering a mutual understanding across countries and cultures. Developments in the delivery of education is allowing for individuals to explore new areas of learning and thinking that could not be done with a pen and paper.

They are discovering knowledge through inquiry and experimentation rather than memorizing facts in a teacher dominated classroom setting. In fact, students no longer need to be physically present to learn as education material is becoming more and more readily available over the internet, through video conferencing, and tape recordings. Institutions are now turning towards the use of the internet to deliver courses to students at a distance and enhance educational programs delivered on campus with increasing frequency. The development of flexible delivery programs is being seen as a significant advancement in the delivery of education.

However, it has been suggested that those students who can explore the vast resources available to them from the comfort of their home will become increasingly impatient with traditional classroom practice. In contrast it is also believed that universal, unlimited, anywhere, anytime access to powerful telecomputers has helped children of all ages "retain their love for learning, improve academic performance and help prepare them for a world in which self-directed lifelong learning is a survival skill". It is thought that students learn better through inquiry and experimentation rather than memorizing facts presented to them by the teacher in a classroom.

A shift in education is becoming evident where more responsibility is being placed on the individual for his or her learning, instead of solely on the teacher. Subsequently, the teacher's role is also changing. Teachers themselves also need to be highly technologically literate, needing the competence and confidence to prepare students for a global information society. Teachers are using technology to empower themselves but are now finding themselves in an education system where they are no longer the sole 'fountain of information' but a facilitator and pointer towards information.

Technology is foreseeing the separation of instructor and learner in time and place for the majority of the instructional process. In an interconnect world, where technology and communication is delivering the world to students, there must be an education curriculum that is both extensive, international and open to new ideas, values and thoughts. The focus needs to be on skills which can be applied to solving global problems and surviving in an ever changing world of shifting circumstances. Education institutions need to provide students with the skills and knowledge required to be productive citizens in a global environment.

A global education should teach about issues that cross national boundaries, and interconnected systems on ecological, cultural, economical, political and technological grounds such as the Globalisation program at Flinders University, South Australia, which draws upon expertise in many areas such as humanities, social science and environmental science.

Globalisation and technological advancements are delivering and increasing access to the world and subsequently subjects should reflect this global outlook as we combine knowledge, creativity and intelligence through electronic connection spanning time and distance. Subsequently, there is a demand for graduates who are highly proficient in dealing with the dramatic scientific, technological and cross cultural changes occurring throughout the world. While there is no "one stop shopping" destination for educational materials on the Internet, ERIC comes close.

The Educational Resources Information Center is a federally funded, nationwide information network designed to provide populations with ready access to educational literature. At the heart of ERIC is the largest education database in the world containing more than 400 000 records of journal articles, research papers, curriculum and teaching guides, conference papers and books. Each year, approximately 30 000 new records are added. More than 30 years ago the ERIC database became available for searching on CD-ROM and is now available through computer networks. It is accessible to teachers, administrators, parents, students, and others through electronic networks including, the Internet, CompuServe, America Online, and other online services throughout the globe. Such databases are changing education significantly. Educationalists throughout the world recognised that they were faced with growing demands for educational provision which could not be met by relying principally upon traditional face-to-face and print based modes of teaching.

The clients are people of all ages, levels of technological sophistication and industries. These clients were requiring education that was appropriate to their needs and often that means independent of time and place. How educationalists can respond to this is was greatly influenced by the evolution of telecommunications networks. The forces shaping the move towards digital media and digital networks were global and manifested to the complex web of cross-sectorial alliances among telephone companies, media firms and computer companies. Such organisations had a profound impact on education providers and their ability to create, package and deliver material to a wide and diverse market.

A cornerstone of this new era is the National Information Infrastructure (NII) which has had an impact on how we work, learn, and entertain ourselves. Although it is in the area of education that the NII has had its most profound effect. Educators and students now have access to online services provided through a combination of commercial and non-commercial providers. The services available today are invaluable and are only getting better as the number and nature of educational offerings expand. Due to these developments educators need no longer be the prime deliverers of "facts". Instead, educators are more like "field guides" as they and their students explore vast domains of knowledge, using the Internet as their trail through the world of information. However, the cost of technology and communication systems has long been an issue of intense discussion, causing many cost/benefit debates within education systems.

While technology and communication developments have been presented as beneficial to education environments, the cost of equipping every student and educator with today's technology is staggering, especially when facing increasingly tight constraints placed on education budgets. However, it can be argued that technology is becoming a lot cheaper when compared to the past, with falling prices making technology educational resources cost competitive with printed materials. Just as technology and communication seems to be creating a divide between the 'haves' and the 'have nots', resulting in a bifurcated society of those who can afford such information technology and those who can't, so too does globalisation.

While education institutions in western societies are embracing technology, developing countries are once again left behind, too weak and fragile to implement development programs for education, let alone introduce technology as well. While third world states encourage their citizens to seek more education, severe limitations in delivering basic services are a problem. A lack of infrastructure and funding makes it difficult to implement any technological and communication advancements into systems that require substantial financial resources where a majority of technology and resources must go to disease prevention and health care.

However, despite differences in economy, polity, culture and society, second and third worlds have adopted educational ideals from western thought and are anxious to appear modern and therefore promote education as a symbol of modernity and development to their own population and the foreign countries. Technology and communication systems will continue to develop and encroach on educational systems worldwide. Globalisation will further drive these changes, presenting new options and challenges to both students and teachers and revolutionize the delivery of education.

However, as the world becomes further and further bifurcated it will be a challenge for education systems to keep up with the development and economic implications of technology, and in particular for developing and third worlds to introduce technology and communication systems into their education infrastructure. However any changes in education through technology and communication will also impact on its delivery and thus have an effect on the receiving culture. Globalisation is a process which has affected many areas of life, one of those being education. In the twentieth century, many developing countries have experienced a growth in the educational facilities available to them due to an influx of institutions from the West. This has raised concerns as to the effect such spreading of education will have on the cultures of the receiving countries. Some believe that this process is an invaluable opportunity for the people of the developing countries to raise their skills and standards of education. Others fear that it is merely a modern version of cultural imperialism that will lead to the creation of a universal, ultimately Western society. From as early as the mid-nineteenth century western countries have been expanding their educational institutions across foreign borders.

The current university institutions in the Indian sub-continent have their origins from the colonial powers. So the current spread of education across international borders is not a new phenomenon. However it is recently that the issue has been raised, as to the effect of this internationalisation of education on cultures. There are two main sides to the argument one side claims that education which moves from Western countries into developing ones is tailored to the needs of the specific culture receiving it.

The other argues that as a result of the globalisation of education, cultures are being taken over by the West in a process of cultural imperialism designed to create a global, essentially Western culture. To begin with I will look at the former argument then follow with a discussion about the latter. One aspect of the globalisation of education has been the creation of 'twinning projects' between one Western and one non-Western university. This results in the creation of a course which is mutually agreed upon and which both institutions can gain from.

The main content of the course is the same but each institution can adapt the material to local needs, resulting in a programme containing an international perspective and local concerns. Such programs do not force the values and beliefs of one culture onto another, but allow both countries to enhance their educational materials whilst ensuring that their culture is nurtured and maintained. One such program exists between the Town of Apatite in e theRussia and the University of Health Sciences in North Sweden.

The aim is to facilitate training and development programs between the two in order to improve institutional care in Russia. The idea is not to force the practices of the Swedish on to the Russians, but to initiate change by the Russian people themselves. People in both countries have realised that "successful change requires the commitment of Russian people rather than the direction by outsiders and for this to happen there needs to be critical reflection so that Russian participants can manage change within a cultural context of Russian society". This is an example of how the process of the globalisation of higher education can be installed and used to both countries' advantage without neglecting the culture of either one.

Educational institutions are "pursuing viable mechanisms and structures for recognizing and accommodating individuals from diverse cultures". He believes that these initiatives usually enhance existing cultures but at the same time realises that we must not lose sight of the "pecking order" since the "adopter" culture must survive at all costs. While he is of the opinion that education systems can and do nurture cultural diversity, he is also aware of the possibility of one culture completely overriding another. This is what some fear will happen, that it will eventually lead to the cultural homogenisation of society into a purely Western one. Education, which is being shipped from the West into developing countries, is intended to improve the skills and capabilities of the people receiving it. But is this process actually responsible for the degradation of the receiving culture? Some have claimed that the United States (one of the countries which transports its education overseas) has been conditioned to think of liberty, equality and opportunity as the birthrights of people everywhere and thus tends to overlook cultural differences. While this can be an advantage, in that they may not discriminate against other cultures, it is a disadvantage when it comes to tailoring education to meet specific cultural needs.

The United States has courses set up all over the world (though only a minority in Third World countries) in an aim to 'enhance the prestige of the university and to broaden the perspectives of students who must be prepared to live in an increasingly interdependent world.' Whilst this may be of advantage to both countries involved, it places no emphasis on the maintenance of the receiving culture. And what exactly do the universities mean when they say "increasingly interdependent world"? Are they referring to the fact that the world is slowly but surely becoming more and more Westernised so that all countries are gaining the same values and beliefs?

Some believe that Westerners tend to be "arrogantly uncritical of the assumptions underlying their teaching and unreflective of the their fitness for teaching across cultures." Cross-border teaching is not as easy as simply going to a country, teaching them a lesson and expecting it to be accepted without question. Different cultures have different values and customs, thus when teaching, the educator needs to be aware of such differences and customise the material accordingly. Isabelle De Courtivron argues that in the United States, which is notoriously a monolingual country, bilingualism is often considered a threat to national unity, and that we need a new form of bilingual and bicultural studies.

The extension of the Western style of education is one that reflects the need of the spreader (very similar to a form of cultural imperialism). This would imply the current spread of higher education into developing countries does not foster the needs of the locals but is done for the benefit of the Western country. Along similar lines, David Orr argues that Western education has in fact replaced "indigenous forms of education throughout the world and focuses on preparing students exclusively for an urban existence." He also claims that through this process, people are losing their vernacular knowledge, by which he means 'the knowledge that people have of their places', that is a loss of their cultural worth. He believes that the modern university does not consider certain aspects of a culture worth knowing other than to record it as an oddity under "folk culture".

Global educators are insensitively spreading their own views of the world onto developing nations in the mistaken belief that they are actually helping people. Such views would imply that the spread of higher education is doing more harm than good because although these people are receiving an education, they are doing so at the cost of their unique culture. It is on this basis that people such as Kell argue for the need for Australian educational institutions to consider linkages which embrace the regional, national and individual needs of the communities which they enter.

The "increasingly transnational character of the study bodies in elite universities are acting as international homogenizing and interacting forces, creating a common identity and culture". This culture they are referring to is essentially Western. In their book, Bull and Watson argue that the transplantation of Western institutions into developing countries shapes the behaviour of those involved and thus makes for greater similarity with the people in which the institutions first evolved.

In fact a study has shown that the process of transferring such institutions results in an increasing similarity of outlooks and values. David Orr believes that "our graduates of tomorrow will be trained, above all, to keep the wheels of the global economy turning". He believes that the Western style of education is inadequate as it focuses largely on the creation of money whilst paying no attention to the preserving of cultures. Many hold the bleak view of the world in the future as one deprived of cultural diversity, where the Western powers will continue to build "educational institutions on their own model as the basis for the expansion of international society", and where non-Western cultures will make only a "very small contribution to that stock of what it is that the middle class culture have in common." The spread of education internationally, as a result of globalisation, has clearly had effects on cultures world wide. However, this is not the only change that can been seen.

The capitalist society is gradually becoming global with a strong emphasis on free-trade emerging. Educational institutions have reacted accordingly, by becoming more market oriented, focussing their energy more on creating funds rather than providing sufficient education for students. The main trade policy developments since the early and mid 1980s have led to greater market orientation and freer trade, under the leadership of the World Trade Organisation, since 1994.

The World Trade Organisation is a forum for harmonising trade conditions around the world. All the members of the World Trade Organisation are committed to all the Multilateral Trade Agreements. In regards to freer trade, in both developed and developing countries tariffs have been significantly reduced, since the establishment of GATT, and more are to be reduced in the near future under the World Trade Agreement. Services trade, such as education, has also been brought into the multilateral system.

Many countries are, as with goods, opening their markets for services trade and investment either unilaterally or through regional or multilateral negotiations. For example, in regards to Australia, there are two Australian studies centres overseas: the Sir Robert Menzies Centre for Australian Studies, University of London; and the Centre for Australian and New Zealand Studies, Georgetown University. Thus, as with goods, services such as education have begun to feel the effects of globalisation of the world economy, in regards to free trade, competitiveness and privatisation. Due to this increasing free trade around the globe - to end protection in many sectors so that there is more competition and privatisation, education is increasingly being drawn into this global capitalist competition.

The underlying philosophy of free trade in international trade agreements (such as the World Trade Agreement) is that, whenever something can be provided by the private sector, conditions should exist so this can occur. Thus, government actions, which obstruct the growth of the private sector, should be identified and destroyed. Because of this 'increasingly dominant neo-liberal environment...universities in the industrialised states were drawn closer to the corporate world.' As well as the World Trade Organisation being established in 1994, at the last round of GATT, the General Agreement on Trade and Services (GATS) was also established. This was the first multilateral agreement on services, as a comprehensive agreement on international trade and services, including education.

Traditionally, trade agreements had been almost solely about reducing tariffs and other trade barriers. It is an extension of the General Agreement on Tariffs and Trade (begun post World War 2) to services, through GATS. The GATS general framework is for no discrimination in favour of national providers. This has been seen in Australia in many sectors, including banking and communication, but now is also evident in education. For example, in the 1999-2000 Australian budget there was a major reform of non-government school funding. Under the rules of GATS 'transparency and progressive liberalism' of services applies to all member countries.

There are a number of GATS specific rules. These include: slight provisions for restrictions on monopolies by the particular government; 'uniform trade policies', that is, consistent trade policies in regards to services throughout the member countries; acknowledgment of foreign professional qualifications; and a reduction in misrepresented subsidies and the like. All of these rules undoubtedly fall under the banner of further liberalisation in regards to services, such as education. Additionally, GATS is administered by the Council for

Trade and Services, which is notified annually of changes in national laws in regards to services such as education. Other member countries are also able to complain to the council about other member's regulations. Thus, there is quite a lot of pressure on member countries of the WTO to conform to this increasing liberalisation of services, such as education.

However, the GATS framework also allows nations to have an individual choice as to what extent services, such as education, are fully open to free trade. Thus, although so far Australia has committed itself to some aspects of free trade in education, it is not yet significantly threatening to public education.

Shortly before the 1999 December Seattle World Trade Organisation meeting the US Trade Ambassador, Charlene Barshefsky announced that the US specifically wanted free trade in education incorporated in the new round of negotiations. Her justifications were purely economic - because much more is achievable in an open market. Thus, this is another example of the recent strong push towards an increasing global and liberalised education system around the world. Both the WTO and one of the leaders in the world economic sphere, the US, are pushing in that direction.

A writer for The Australian, believes that public universities in Australia will be the 'last great socialist enterprise' to be thrown into the open market. He believes that this will create greater efficiency, as the sector needs 'the discipline of the market to get it into shape. Thus, like other government enterprises that have been privatised, education will become a lot more competitive if in an open market system. Additionally, he believes that education, where possible, should be integrated into the private sector because 'higher education is increasingly an international enterprise' and thus will increasingly be pressured and drawn into deregulation and privatisation. This can be seen in regards to GATS, which is increasingly calling for countries to greater liberalise services such as education. At the very least he believes that, like other recent privatisation and deregulation of government sectors, such as communication, there will be a system in the education sector where public institutions compete on an equal footing with private ones, due to equal access to public funds. We can already see this starting to occur in Australia, with the 1999-2000 budget reform of funding to non-government schools. Thus, some commentators, like Schwartz, believe that open market education is inevitable, and definite signs are already being seen in that direction.

There are many elements currently present that indicate that education is already emeshed in the world's free trade and competitive philosophy. Firstly, there is cross border supply. This is where the provider of education and the buyer do not move, for example, delivering education across the world through satellite broadcasting. Secondly, in regards to consumption abroad, there is a commercial presence of foreign investors in many host countries. For example, foreign universities are setting up courses or institutions in other countries. Thirdly, there is commercial presence, that is, where the provider establishes a physical presence in the host country. Lastly, there is the presence of persons who leave their country to study or provide education abroad. For example, academics on short-term contracts and international students in Australia. However, there are still some barriers to these four modes of delivery in regards to the globalisation of education present. For example, there are national requirements to set up an institution or courses and to receive government grants. Additionally, there are government monopolies. Moreover, there are direct restrictions on students, for example, immigration and visa requirements.

However, if the new round of negotiations at the World Trade Organisation succeeds in eliminating the barriers to complete free trade in education, the 'private sector will receive enormous power to undermine the public delivery of education services'. Thus education has been effected by the globalisation of the world economy, especially in regards to free trade and privitisation to a moderate extent, but there is much more potential for it to develop even more in the near future. Thus, through GATS, the World Trade Organisation, enthusiasm from individual governments, such as the current Australian Liberal Government, as well as pushes from the US, education is being increasingly drawn into the new global, free and competitive world of economics.

There are already many examples of this. For example, cross border supply, consumption abroad, a commercial presence of foreign investors in education, as well as a presence of international students in host countries. There seems to also be a lot of potential for education to be even more correlated in this system in years to come, with increasing calls and pushes in that direction from the World Trade Organisation and powerful countries around the world, such as the US. Due to the increase in multilateral agreements and free trade practices in regards to education, education can also be said to be internationalised. Not only are universities having to compete on a global scale, but they are also becoming more competitive and entrepreneurial. In this way education can be said to be commodified in this increasingly capitalist world. "The Internationalisation of education has become one of the key themes of educational policy and planning in the 1990s.

In an era typified by the globalisation of technology, communications, and the integration of worldwide capital and labour markets, educators are being forced to respond to a new set of challenges." The Internationalisation of Education can be given many definitions. It can be described as integration of culture into teaching methods or processes by which education becomes more internationally orientated. However perhaps a better description is " the process that prepares the community for successful participation in an increasingly interdependent world, fosters global understanding and develops skills for effective living, working in a diverse world."

The internationalisation of education, particularly higher education, is a growing phenomenon. Universities and colleges around the world are increasingly becoming forced to compete in the global capitalist market and engage in entrepreneurial activity to sustain themselves in an increasingly ' uncertain world '. Universities are no longer always state controlled and are, more often than not, controlled by transnational companies carrying names like Microsoft Corporation. Government's support universities that market themselves internationally as it provides education locally whilst at the same time creating revenue.

Education, in this sense, has literally become ' commodified'. But, is this commodity accessible to all, including people in developing countries? Is the structure of education changing to survive on the ' open market '? The internationalisation of higher education can be linked to various internal and external changes in the international system. Externally, there have been changes in the labour market, which have resulted in calls for more knowledged and skilled workers, and workers with deeper understandings of languages, cultures and business methods from all over the world."

Modern education...is almost exclusively focused on preparing children for an urban future, as consumers in a global ' free' market." Due to this ' internationalisation ', educational institutions are being encouraged by governing authorities and transnational corporations to ' market ' themselves overseas. At this point, it is interesting to note that Australian universities are still generating millions in tuition from foreign students. In terms of foreign student numbers, Australia is ranked third after the United States and Britain. How do Universities become 'internationalised'? What educational strategies are put in place to internationalise long-standing curriculum of higher education institutions? Universities market their courses " with an international orientation in content, aimed at preparing students for performing (professionally/socially) in an international and multicultural context."

Internationalising education means courses and topics, either existing or new, must be delivered in a global capacity which naturally means via the Internet and online. Coping with this technology requires huge amounts of time and money, not to mention expertise and skilled workers to deal with the technology. Tragically, Government funding to universities is suffering massive cutbacks leaving many long-standing institutions with little money, yet they are still expected to compete ' globally '. In order to attract foreign students and therefore foreign revenue, universities must provide the global consumer with what is demanded. Courses must be flexible, adaptable, online and above all, interactive between the various cultures around the world. For universities, the internationalisation of education doesn't come easily. The internationalisation of education almost gives the impression that the educational institution is no longer in control. In order to survive, universities rely on the business of domestic and foreign students.

These students in turn make their decision on which institution to attend by the way their courses are marketed. Unbeknown to the prospective students, universities face many problems in the new race to become a successful competitor on the global market. With the availability of online courses, will there eventually be no need for lecturers or academics? Will research and development be reduced and will courses become more generalised? With flexible delivery of lectures via the Internet, will universities not only require course specialists but also information technology experts? Flexible delivery then means that universities must compete with each other locally, as well as globally.

In the absolute extreme, will internationalisation of education mean that students can learn from the home via the Internet thus rendering universities, in a physical sense, as no longer necessary? Worse still, is education becoming a capitalist enterprise " wherein learning ceases to be about analysis, discussion and examination, and becomes a product to be bought and sold, to be packaged, advertised and marketed? " Current trends would suggest that this is becoming a reality. Education is bought and is therefore certainly sold and marketed. What about the quality of the product? A critique of the 'modern' education system can be found in David Orr's " Education for Globalisation." Orr suggests that the newly internationalised education prepares students almost exclusively for " an urban existence, and dependence on fossil fuel and global trade. Children are taught from an early age how best to compete." Orr argues that students are not being taught how best to live in a sustainable society.

Quality of education is being replaced with quantity. Modern western education today " emphasises theories instead of values, concepts rather than human beings, abstraction rather than consciousness, answers instead of questions, ideology and efficiency rather than conscience." Orr then argues that these practices are driving the planet to the point of crisis rather than sustenance. Perhaps Orr's strongest argument comes in the form of " The Six Myths of Modern Education." Orr laments that with the rate at which society is becoming globalised and ' internationalised ', we are losing values, our sense of self and basic humanity. Advancing technologies go hand in hand with growing ignorance to some of the basic aspects of life. There is an overriding sense that western culture represents the pinnacle of human achievement and this is perhaps one of the worst forms of cultural arrogance.

Globalisation of the world economy and globalisation of education does in fact lead to this arrogance, does it not? Western capitalism should not perceive itself as such a pinnacle however, because it destroys morality. " Capitalism has also failed because it produces too much and shares too littie, also at too high a cost to our children and grandchildren."

Modern education is focused almost entirely on continuing the processes of globalisation, where " the graduates of tomorrow will be trained, above all, to keep the wheels of the global economy turning, with all the implications that has for nature and society." To get down to the business of education, it is hardly surprising that since modern and 'internationalised' education produces urban consumers, that business is taking interest in how educational institutions are being run. Corporate interests are reshaping education in accordance with it's own "profit chasing interests." An example of such activity is Channel One TV in America, which exchanges free TV to school students, for the right to screen two minutes of commercial advertising during the school day.

A prime example of the impact that globalisation has an education. This sort of entrepreneurial activity pushes students in the direction of a globalised, technocratic, consumeristic, fragmented world, when instead we need people to repair the damage that the world has done. What about the extension of western-style education into the non-western world? Access to higher education remains one of the great inequalities in today's global community.

The 'internationalisation' of education and therefore its globalisation, is carrying the "full ensemble of western institutions to much of the developing world." Together with this and the decline of international economic aid, there has been a considerable amount of underpinning for university development in the poorer countries. The role of education has become more linked to globally competitive positions. Subsequent changes in university functions have lead universities toward" direct entrepreneurial activity to sustain themselves." This in turn produces a change in institutional approaches to the development of overseas education.

University courses must now be cross-cultural in content, which is in association with the growing number of students, particularly in the 1990's, searching for higher education outside of their own country. It is estimated that "by the year 2025, the world's post secondary institutions will be expected to accommodate some 200 million students." This is compared to 82 million in 1995. It is also a fact that domestic and foreign full-fee paying students will make up the majority of this predicted number.

The World Declaration for Higher Education for the Twenty-First Century has reflected a commitment to provide "access to higher education...based on the merit of the individual." This raises on interesting question. In a rapidly expanding educational system, how affordable can higher education be? Access to higher education is a right, it should not be limited to ' the better off ' due to inability to pay. Education is becoming more invaluable to individuals as society changes to cope in a globalising world. In today's environment, education provides individuals with a better chance of employment, which in turn leads to a better lifestyle, power and status. In an ' internationalised' society, " globalisation of education (depends) upon the existence of classes able to pay." Education, particularly full-fee education" is an expensive commodity ", those who receive it are regarded as being ' better off '.

The internationalisation of education leads to the distribution of future status and power. Western institutions conveying their interests overseas by marketing ' our ' universities is rather like " selling a standard product that is marketed as being the right product for all occasions." The need to sell education overseas is increasingly being interpreted as " a lifeline for higher education and vocational training providers squeezed by shrinking government education budgets ". Universally, higher education has become an extremely competitive enterprise on the global capitalist market.

The better the university is at marketing themselves, the bigger the profits it will make. Whatever happened to ' free ' education? Globalisation happened, that's what. Globalisation has had many obvious effects on education. As globalisation progresses, we will continue to see many changes in the structure and content of the education system internationally. Technology and communication systems change the way education is delivered as well as roles played by both teachers and students.

The development of this technology is facilitating the transition from an industrial based society to an information based one. The delivery of education has become more of a global process thus raising questions as to the effects on cultures world wide. There has been suggestions that the globalisation of education is a new form of western cultural imperialism. As a result of world moves toward free trade, the 'commodification' of education has emerged , thus rendering educational institutions as profit making enterprises. This has led to international concerns about the affordability and accessibility of the commodity. Globalisation has transformed education and will continue to do so, leaving us with a future that is more unpredictable than ever.

Globalisation and the Future of Education

We seek here to answer the following question: How will education -particularly in Latin America- be affected by the changes that are occurring outside it. This text is divided into four parts.

The first part briefly describes, from different points of view, existing perceptions in Latin America regarding education at the beginning of the XXI century:

— From the point of view of the intelligentsia and the media;

— From the point of view of people and civil associations, and

— From the point of view of education specialists and of people who influence education policy.

The resulting picture is essentially contradictory. Above all, the great expectations announced do not appear to be compatible with the negative development of an environment that is predicted to result in globalization. The second part analyzes globalization as a context from the viewpoint of the thesis that argues that it is the direct or indirect cause of a large variety of frequently negative effects for the development of education within countries. We seek to verify the explanatory ability of this thesis from the viewpoint of the "impact propensity of global interconnectivity" which distinguishes four analytically distinct types of impacts of globalization: decisional, institutional, distributive, and structural. When submitted to this analysis, the "grand effects" thesis appears to be unjustified, however.

Rather, we suggest here that over-representation of such effects may be due to the use of hermeneutic devices that exaggerates them or accuses globalization - as a background context - to be the immediate cause of a variety of consequences of very dissimilar origin. In the third part, we advance the hypothesis that globalization, as a background phenomenon, has an impact on the immediate and proximate contexts within which education develops, changing them significantly. We propose five proximate and relevant context dimensions for education, in which important changes are taking place and which represent challenges for education in the XXI century:

— Access to information,

— Store house for knowledge

— Labor market

— Availability of new technologies for education, and

— Socialization for "diverse world realities".

— The fourth and last part is dedicated to exploring the way that developed countries seek to adjust their education systems to changes in their immediate surroundings. We suggest that there are three basic strategies that - combined together - are in course:

— Toward life-long learning for all;

— Toward distance education and distributed learning, and

— Toward the inst itutionalization of networks

In each case, we analyze what operations are being put in place in order to develop these strategies and what objectives they obey. Finally, in a concluding section, we note that Latin American education confronts two enormous challenges. On the one hand, to fulfill pending tasks of the XX century such as offering universal pre-school, basic, and secondary coverage; incorporate indigenous populations into the school system; improve the quality of learning outcomes for basic skills, particularly among the most economically disadvantaged groups of infants, juveniles, and adults; modernize secondary and higher-level technical education; general access to higher education.

On the other hand, we should advance toward the XXI century and embark on the new tasks on which economic development, social equity, and cultural integration depend, adapting for this purpose structures, processes, and results to education policy, to transformations that, due to globalization, are part of the contexts of information, knowledge, work, technology, and cultural meaning in which teaching and learning processes develop. Both agendas - of the XX century and of the XXI century- are tremendously demanding and costly. To apply them at the same time is a feat that requires considerable effort. Adjusting their ends and implementation rates will, from here on, be the key for education policies. The risks that appear in these circumstances are commensurate with the magnitude of the challenges.

Perceptions at the Beginning of the Century

In spite of improvements witnessed by the region during the second half of the XX century, a question persists in regard to whether Latin America will one day become a developed continent. Currently, the words that best express the feelings of Latin American authorities and intellectuals in regard to the future are those such as "doubt", "bewilderment", "confusion", or "ambiguity", as if, in truth, the ground had begun to move under everyone and it is not clear where we are heading.

To the mediocre results of the last decade of the XX century - only 3% economic growth, just one point more than during the "lost decade" of the 1980s; with 44% of the population living in poverty, 19% in absolute poverty, and with the worse income distribution of any world region—are now added the emerging challenges of the technology revolution and of globalization. All of this in the middle of democracies that are weakly institutionalized, markets that operate excluding large groups of the population, cultural identities that appear to be threatened, and a fourth sector - made up of the informal economy, black market, and criminal culture (drug traffic, guerilla, urban crime) - the perverse advance of which seems unstoppable.

There really are no reasons to be optimistic in Latin America; nor should one exaggerate the feeling of unrest and threat in the face of the future. Very well: education is at this cross-roads. Between mediocre results and enormous challenges; caught between unsolved problems of the XX century and new ones to appear in the XXI century.

In spite of reform efforts during the past decades and more public spending on education - which increased by 22% between 1990 and 1996 and then continued to increase until the end of the decade - education remains backward on the regional level - underdeveloped, or semi-underdeveloped in the best of cases.

With insufficient coverage and serious levels of exclusion in some countries; low capacit y to compensate for cultural deprivation of children from poor households; high rates of grade repetition and drop-out that translate into high rates of waste; unsatisfactory learning results; limited and habitually badly managed and/or utilized human resources within the education system; poor articulation between levels of the system and of the system as a whole with the environment, particularly with the labor market; low education levels in the over 25 year-old work force (a 5 year average) and 14% of the population illiterate; pronounced differences in terms of years of schooling of the population between the 10% richest (11 years or more) and the 30% poorest (less than 4 years); low production of knowledge in order to improve teaching and learning processes and to provide input for public policies for this sector, etc.

In its turn, the perceptions of major actors regarding the state of education comprise a complex picture, with convergent and divergent elements of diagnoses and expectations. From the point of view of the upper class, the intelligentsia and the media, education appears to be placed at the center of national development debate; almost as an answer - situated, apparently, beyond ideology, although in fact it begins to operate as a new, "neutral" and "consensual" ideology - in the face of the great questions of the XXI century.

Suddenly, beginning in the 1980s, governments, authorities, intellectuals, and the mass media - together with international agencies such as UNESCO, the OECD, World Bank, and the Inter-American Development Bank, began to identify education as the major instrument for the development of countries, economic growth, increases of productivity, and to overcome, or at least narrow the internal gap of poverty and the external one of knowledge and technology that separates developed and developing countries. There is more: education is seen as a (or the) principal ingredient to re-establish social cohesion, avoid juvenile anomie, prevent crime and drug addiction, affirm societal values, etc.

From the point of view of popular perception and of social groups, in turn, education appears as one of the most precious social goods, if not the most powerful means to attain individual and collective well-being. In effect, people demonstrate a growing respect for the role that education plays in current conditions of society to prosper materially and to gain social mobility. Thus, for example, the latest version of the Latinbarómetro (2000) shows that in Latin America (17 countries), some 60% of population feel that "the most important thing to be successful in life is education"; against 19% who opt for "hard work", 12% for "connections", and 8% "luck".

Similarly, various grouping with society, cultural organizations and social movements throughout the region - as well as progressive and conservative politicians (although at times for contrary reasons) declare that education has a relevant role in training for a new citizenship, community cohesion, the dissemination of positive social values, the preservation of local and national identity, the development of a feeling of collective protection in the face of the market, self-awareness regarding human rights, care for the environment, etc. From the point of view of education specialists (from inside and outside the region) and of people who influence education policy decisions, we see an ambiguous picture of ideas and perceptions regarding the future of education in Latin America.

As a study conducted by Schwartzman (2000) shows, both segments expect for the next 15 years "a clearly negative environment" in which education systems must be developed:

— An "adverse economic context", characterized by stagnation and low growth as well as a scarcity of public resources to be used for social policy, including budgets for basic education;

— A "negative social context", characterized by growing exclusion and social inequality due to restructuring that will take place in societies under the pressure of globalization and the increasingly intensive use of knowledge and technology.

Nevertheless, at the same time, representatives of both groups predict that during this time period:

— There will be increased interest in education on the part of society, accompanied by a greater mobilization of resources in its favor, with a positive effect on the development of the system;

— Education will play an important role in promoting citizenship, creating a more just social order, and furnish necessary basic life skills;

— Furthermore, it will play a highly positive role in reducing inequalities within countries in the region.

How can specialists and those who influence education policies imagine that education can produce such positive results in a context characterized by them as being so negative? Among the answers recorded by Schwartzman (2000) one cannot find a satisfactory answer to this question. In effect, the negative context is not expected to change - to neutralize the effects or make them favorable - nor is it thought that it will be possible to take advantage of opportunities to move education forward.

Thus, although both groups consulted - specialists and the influential - believe that the new information and communication technologies (NICT) will transform education, they do not believe that these technologies will serve to overcome the gap that separates us from the developed countries. Nor, moreover, to overcome education differences within countries between urban and rural areas.

Nor do specialists agree with the idea that continuing education can be a change agent in the current situation, opening new learning opportunities for the population and lead to a redefinition of the school system. Nor do the believe that, faced with expected changes in context, teacher training and the teaching profession will undergo significant changes in the future. The only factors upon which specialists and the influential agree in regard to the organization and functioning of future schools are:

— The trend toward greater organizational decentralization and management of education systems, including higher degrees of local autonomy and community participation, all of which is seen as highly positive;

— The trend toward more intense use of quantitative assessment methods of teacher and student performance as a means of guiding public policies, and

— The trend toward universal access to pre-school programs which are hoped to serve to significantly improve basic and secondary education.

From the point of view of specialists and the influential, there is skepticism in regard to changes in the environment within which education will function in the near future; but not so in terms of some dynamics of system transformation .- such as decentralization - and even less in regard to its expected effects, in which full optimism reigns. In effect, it is expected that education will produce positive political impacts (the citizenship effect) and social impacts (the equity effect). But, in general, the picture one has of this exercise of imagining the future of education in Latin America seems to be essentially contradictory.

The Context of Globalisation

As for the environment within which education will develop, the published literature during the last decade 6 agrees in at least this: that it is changing - rapidly and profoundly - to the point of becoming unrecognizable to XX century eyes. The most general thesis presented in this regard says that globalization will have impacts on that environment in multiple and varied ways, modifying it substantially. In spite being widely disseminated and repeated, it is not, however, a clear and defined thesis. Most commonly it is formulated without defining the meaning of "globalization" or offering measures of the extent (generally negative) of the postulated effects.

Usually, in effect, globalization is defined as the growing integration of national economies. At its core, the global economy would include the globalization of financial markets, "the behavior of which determines the movement of capital, currency, credit, and, therefore, the economies of all countries". But, in addition, one hears of the globalization of science, of technology, of information; the globalization of communication and culture; the globalization of politics; even the globalization of organized crime.

It behooves us, therefore, to define the reach of the term that we are going to employ during this article and to ask how globalization affects education. The question for us here, however, is what are the (pertinent) impacts of globalization, and what effects they produce within the area of education systems and policies. A "generalist" definition of globalization - constructed, moreover, to take into account its effects - is that provided by Held et.al., according to which the phenomenon may be understood as "the process or processes that embody "change in the organizational space of social relations and transactions, generating transcontinental and inter-regional flows and networks of activities, inter-action, and exercise of power ..." The suggestion of these authors is that forms and degrees of progress of globalization may be described and compared in regard to four spatial-temporal dimensions: the "extensiveness" of global networks in terms of connections and relations; "intensity" of flows and levels of activity within such networks; "velocity" of exchanges, and the "impact" of such phenomena on particular communities. It is the latter dimension that interests us here.

The impact propensity of global interconnectedness" by distinguishing four analytically distinct types of impact of globalization: decisional, institutional, distributive, and structural. The first two kinds of impact tend to be direct, but they may also cause indirect effects, while the last two types usually operate in an indirect manner. In short, "decisional impacts" have to do with the degree in which globalization processes alter the costs and benefits relative to various policy options taken by governments, corporations, groups, or households. In turn, "institutional impacts" have to do with the way that forces and conditions of globalization determine the agenda of available options for policy-makers.

"Distributional impacts", for their part, are related to the form in which globalization influences the configuration of social forces (groups, classes, collectives) within societies and between countries. Finally, "structural impacts" of globalization are those that determine in the short, medium, and long term the organizational standards and political, economic, and social behavior of a society as a product of the conflicts that are generated around adapting to or resisting the forces of globalization.

A review of the literature on globalization and education carried out using this analytic scheme offers a good starting point for discussion. In effect, it allows us to see that most studies and articles attribute to globalization a series of impacts of the four kinds mentioned above, at the same time that, in reality, the arguments used in such studies and articles are not able to demonstrate how in each case the predicated decisional, institutional, distributional, and structural effects are produced.

Practically everything the currently happens in education, as well as in regard to orientation, direction, and implementation of education reform policies and processes appears to be linked - by some author at some time - to the phenomenon of globalization, although only at times is a cause/ effect relation proven. One may assert that this high propensity of the impact attributed to globalization in education is due, above all, to the use of certain "hermeneutic devices" that exaggerate its effects or allege that globalization - as a background context - is the immediate cause of a variety of consequences of dissimilar origin.

One of these devices - among the most used - is the "ideological over-determination of globalization" that consists in judging it to have a single ideological orientation (neo-liberal). Such an orientation is then alleged to have an effect on education and on education policies. Here is an example: I argue that globalization is having a profound effect on education at many levels. I agree that educational decentralization is a major manifestation, if not of globalization itself, certainly of an ideology closely identified with and pushing the development of the global economy in a particular direction. So we need to ask how this larger ideological package, that includes but is not limited to decentralization, affects education".

Another typical feature is that of "causal linking" - when, for example, it is claimed that globalization "has tended to undermine the welfare states on which universities depended for the bulk of their income", wishing to thus indicate that globalization is responsible, in the last analysis, for the drop in public funding for public universities. This is the same argument used to "explain" a supposed decline in resources that the State provides to education in general.

A third device consists in using globalization "a general and immediate cause" taking for granted that it operates by itself in a direct fashion as the cause of a series of (general adverse) phenomena that affect education. For example: "economic opportunities generated by globalization make the teaching profession, in relative terms, even less attractive, diminishing the quality of teachers.

The demands of globalization increase pressures on the education system form groups with the greatest political power, increasing inequality and segregation in schools. They increase violence, instability, and political conflict, which acts negatively on the education system. It produces the removal of teachers and students (the case of Colombia, currently), instability in the financing of education, and difficulties in adopting a long-range perspective in the management of educatio.

The most frequently-used device is certainly that of the "elective affinity effects" between globalization, neo-liberal ideas, and certain correspondence effects, correlation, proximity, similarity, relationship, parallelism, or harmony produced in the education system such as: educational productionism, deterioration of working conditions for teachers, privatization, assessment pressures, international comparisons of performance, decentralization, etc. For example, Pereyra et al introduce their book stating that, "globalization and decentralization are two terms constructed and reaffirmed in social science discourse and in public discourse during the 1980s. Controversial concepts, very politically active and not at all fleeting, they reflect the creation of a world society defining the change of the times in which we live".

It is not surprising that the principal problem, or weakness, of the "grand effects" thesis lies in saying that globalization - as a background context - is the immediate cause of a variety of consequences in the field of education or in education policy; consequences that undoubtedly are of quite dissimilar origins. In effect, to be in the background does not cause anything. Thus, for example, the decentralization of education may obey various causes and follow different paths in different societies without the background globalization process having any importance.

The same is the case with the decrease or increase of public funding of education, with greater or lesser presence of competitive elements in the system, with the privatization of education, etc. In any case, what is most certain is that empirical analysis shows that these are cases of phenomena that are still dictated, essentially, by what one author calls the rule of "methodological nationalism"; that is, that the limits of society are considered to be coincident with those of the nation State, and serve as a "holder" of the particular phenomena that one seeks to explain. In short, the grand effects theory does not provide an adequate means to assess the consequences of globalization on the environment within which education develops, and thus to assess the consequences of the changes in said environment on the insides of the education system; that is, on the processes of teaching and learning.

Who is one of the authors who most intelligently develops the "grand effects" thesis, recognizes this weakness when he states, "it is true that education seems to have changed little at the classroom level in most countries - even in those countries most involved in the global economy and in the information era. Besides the occasional use of computers in the classroom, teaching methods and national curricula remain practically untouched. Even one of the most important education reforms associated with globalization - decentralization in the management and financing of education - seems to have little or no impact on the delivery of education within the classroom the form in which such delivery is made in the classroom is an important aspect of the production of knowledge, and that classrooms appear to be basically untouched. But that is only one part of the process of the production of knowledge and, moreover.

The question is whether it wouldn't be possible to offer a better-fitting interpretation of the effects of globalization on education. To do so, instead looking at it as a background cause that operates through "elective affinities", it should be treated as a part of the environment within which education develops, affecting relevant dimensions of the contexts within which it operates and to which it must respond and adopt. With this, we will here understand by "globalization" essentially the processes that result in the dissemination of NICT - particularly network technologies - and we will seek to define to what extent they are changing the proximate contexts within which education should develop. We propose five context dimensions within which the on-going transformations are important and, consequently, represent challenges for education in the XXI century:

— Access to information
— Storehouse of knowledge
— Labor market
— Availability of NTIC for education
— Worlds of life

Access to Information

An important part of education has to do with

information: about the world around us, about others, and about ourselves. Granted that information is not exactly the same as knowledge (we will, in fact, treat both separately), but neither should we exaggerate the distinction. "Knowledge" always involves information (although it goes further) and, on the other hand, the management of information over knowledge is of growing importance. We know that throughout history, information has been scarce and difficult to access. Ever since the invention of writing, the richest information has been found in texts which were only accessible to a small minority even up to the 19th century, during which illiteracy levels were still extraordinarily high throughout the world. The invention of the printing press produced a veritable revolution by making the writing within texts easy to reproduce. Still, it was some time before books and magazines were available to the masses, and only in the last few decades have we seen a real explosion. Thus, for example, while the Harvard University Library took 275 years to collect its first million books, the last million only took 5 years.

Today, the situation of available and accessible information is completely different. It is increasingly more abundant and easy to obtain, as witnessed by the internet and www. As Fenwick, the Education Director of AT&T has pointed out, it is expected that by the year 2002, there will be 8 billion electronic pages per day. This is currently growing at a rate of 2 million pages per day. The people who access the internet, who still represent a minority in the world, are highly concentrated in northern countries. This number is steadily growing. It is estimated that the number will reach 1 billion within the next 10 years.

In Latin America, the number of people who currently access the internet is 13 million, and is expected to increase to 30 million by the end of 2003. Therefore, the problem for education currently is not where to find information, but how to offer access without excluding , and how to teach, learn, select, assess, interpret, classify, and use the information. There is an additional question involved here: how to develop the "higher cognitive functions of "problem-solving, problem-finding, planning, reflecting, creativity, deeper understanding" -that are indispensable within a medium saturated with information, and avoiding that education be reduced to the level of basic or elementary skills.

Thus, schools are no longer the principal source of information for the new generation, but must compete with other mediums such as television and the internet, the use of which, one hopes, will inform and teach.

Knowledge

Education is more than the transmission and acquisition of knowledge and cultivation of logical-mathematical intelligence. It involves values, develops practices and behaviors, forges character, recognizes the formative role of the emotions in learning processes, seeks to foster the maturation of multiple intelligences, and permits students to explore and utilize their own abilities in every possible dimension. Even so, transmitted and acquired knowledge constitutes an essential dimension of the entire educational process. Not long ago, this function of inculcation of knowledge was favored by the fact that the global platform of knowledge, and the bases of disciplinary knowledge, were relatively small and stable. This facilitated the task of schools.

— Today, on the other hand, knowledge increases and changes very rapidly. This may be illustrated with examples taken from various disciplines:

— *Chemistry*: since the beginning of the 1990s, more than 1 million articles have appeared in specialized journals every 2 years. Between 1978 and 1988, the number of known substances went from 360,000 to 720,000 - reaching 1.7 million in 1998

— *Biology*: Only in 1977 was a method designed to determine the base sequence (the letters that codify the information of DNA); initially, it was possible to determine the sequence of 500 bases per week. Today, this same method, perfected and automated, can decipher the 3 billion bases of the human genome in a few years. Presently, a genome center can determine a million bases per day.

— Mathematics: 100,000 new theorems are created per year.

— *History*: the discipline produced in two decades - between 1060 and 1980 -more publications than in the entire previous period since classical Greece.

— Management: in recent years, this area has produced five books per day.

Considered together, it is estimated that knowledge (the disciplinary base published and recorded internationally) had taken 1,750 years to double, calculating from the beginning of the Christian era. It then doubled in volume, successively, in 150 years, 50 years, and now, every 5 years. It is estimated that by the year 2020, it will double ever 73 days. Under these conditions, according to Gardner, "the individual (or "intelligent agent") who can examine these bodies of knowledge and determine what is worth knowing will be at a tremendous premium. Even more estimable will be the person (or browser) who (or that) can synthesize the exponentially expanding domains of knowledge so that vital information can be made available in useful form to the average citizen and the average policymaker".

All of this presents serious challenges to education systems and to schools in particular. Who will be the synthesizers of knowledge of tomorrow? What other areas will be added to the concept of "basic skills" (computers, net surfing, use of multi-media), when, and in what modalities? In terms of curriculum, how can we organize global knowledge that is constantly changing and growing? What do we do with the fact that a growing proportion of relevant knowledge is trans-disciplinary? How much emphasis should be placed in education on disciplines?

Changes in the labour market

Throughout history, education has fulfilled the function of preparing people for exercising adult roles; particularly for entering the labor market. It is often argued today that globalization has carried this to a perverse extreme (the grand effect thesis!), placing upon education a utilitarian, business-oriented function that is no more than the mere training of the labor force. Be that as it may, it is evident that education here faces an accelerated change in context. Increasing numbers of people are employed in a service sector in which one of the entrance requirements is to have acquired necessary inter-personal skills.

Certain occupations demand increasingly higher levels of schooling and reward increasing levels accordingly, and thus increasing the distance between those who have less and those who have more schooling. In general, a growing number of jobs require that people know how to read and understand technical information. The same is the case for the requirement to be computer-literate. Moreover, people now need to be trained for unstable career paths and to expect not only probable changes of employers, but changes in occupation and economic sector as well.

In a deeper sense, we raise a question here of a structural nature in terms of future relations between education and labor. As Bertrand notes, the link between the economy, technological, and organizational development, has various consequences for the job-readiness of people and their education and training. First, changes are taking place in job structures; that is, in the distribution of occupations between different sectors. We have mentioned the increase of activity in the service sector and the decrease of jobs in agriculture, extractive industry, and assembly. We should also note the disappearance of certain intermediate activities and industries that have been replaced by direct contact between providers and users or clients on the net; the increase of engineers and technicians; the strong development of symbolic analysts which we will refer to below; the increase of occupations in the service sector, and the perverse growth of the fourth sector; and mass unemployment, etc. In the case of the highest-income countries in Latin America, we see: in increase of non-manual occupations and a reduction in jobs in agriculture; an increase of highly-qualified professionals and of technicians; a decrease in the number of people in the commercial sector; greater participation of personal service workers.

In second place, the work content of occupations is rapidly changing in many cases, generating new demands for abilities, skills, and knowledge. Not only are more skills needed; frequently those required are new and different, which places education and professional training systems in check.

Bertrand and others similar ones that abound in the literature on contemporary organizations and the nature of more dynamic occupations disregard a fact. This is that - as Robert Reich asked almost a decade ago - the global world of labor is moving toward a three-part division in which:

— At the basis are "routine production services" (blue-collar workers, but also low and mid-level managerial positions), in which repetition and the control of automatic tasks are important. This kind of activity exists widely in the industrial sector (including NICT) and in services. It requires a basic education, and above all, trustworthiness, loyalty, the ability to follow instructions, and punctuality.

— On the intermediate level we find "in-person services" also comprising simple and routine client service tasks in which women predominate, such as tasks carried out in sales, waiters, fast-food restaurant workers, sales check-out, hospital assistants, secretaries, hair dressers, mechanics, security guards, etc. Here the maximum required education would be the equivalent of complete high school, plus some vocat ional orientation; and

— On the higher level we find "symbolic-analytic services", which include highly-trained people who identify, solve, and/or arbitrate solutions for complex problems through the manipulation of symbols such as scientific researchers, computer and sound engineers, RRPP executives, investment bankers, management and tax consultants, architecture, urbanism, information systems, energy, armaments, specialists in organizational development, strategic planning, industrial strategies, etc.

The idea, then, that, due to demands arising from the economic structure and from technological and organizational change, education requirements for employment will be raised for all and for all segments of the labor market, does not seem to be substantiated in the observable development of the world labor market. Some may think, then, that we may be producing "excessive education" from the point of view of requirements of the economy. There are even those who argue that developing countries - especially in the export of low added-value natural resources - it really makes no sense to insist upon indiscriminately raising the education level of the population.

In fact, recent developments in the Latin American labor market show a trend toward relatively rigid segmentation, both in terms of income as well as in terms of education level of the labor force - higher, intermediate, and lower - that represent approximately 3%, 20%, and 74% of the economically active population. The upper level encompasses professionals with an average of 15 years of education.

The intermediate level includes directors and managers, technicians, administrative employees, and business people, whose average education levels fluctuate between a minimum of 8.9 years and a maximum of 12.1 of study. At the lower level, that includes sales workers, laborers, craftspeople, drivers, and those occupied in personal services and in agriculture. The level of instruction at this level in urban areas fluctuates between 5.5 and 7.3 years of study. In rural areas, these numbers reach only 2.9 years.

On the contrary, there are those who argue - also from the economic point of view - that investing strongly in education, above all in countries whose development is led by the extraction of natural resources, is a pre-requisite, in order to foster greater development from the point of view of knowledge and technologies, adding value to exports and generating new economic activities in more dynamic and technologically-intensive sectors.

In any case, it should be remembered that by the end of the XX century, the demand for education had ceased to be driven exclusively - and sometimes not even principally - by economic considerations. The fact is, education has gradually acquired greater autonomy in regard to purely material considerations and has entered the sphere of post-materialist aspirations: as a citizen right, as a form of consumption and use of free time, as a means of personal self-discovery, community contact, therapeutic support, or participation in the culture of the times, etc.

Where education does appear to be closely linked to participation in the global labor market is in the segment that Reich calls that of the "symbolic analysts". This, indeed is the highest possible level of education, although not necessarily expressed through the usual academic diplomas, nor manifested through the classic notion of a professional career. The symbolic analyst, rather, operates on the cutting-edge. "For in the new economy, replete with unidentified problems, unknown solutions, and unproven means to unite both, the mastery of the traditional domains of knowledge is no guarantee for successful entry. Nor is it necessary.

Symbolic analysts can frequently take advantage of bodies of established knowledge simply through touching a computer keyboard. Facts, codes, formulas, and rules are easily accessible. What is more valuable is the ability to creatively and effectively use such knowledge. The possession of a professional credential is no guarantee for this. Indeed, professional education that has emphasized the memorization of knowledge in detriment to the development of original thought may retard such capacity later on". In this context, Flores and Gray speak of the "end of the career", of the structure that until now has organized the link between higher education and professional employment for the most-educated segment of society. It is true that the symbolic analyst lacks a professional career , an stable occupational path, and even an identity organized around his or her profession. It is even necessary to resort to linguistic artifices in order to "name" the occupation and to capture something of the halo of a title- for status.

The names that Reich suggests, with a touch of irony, are the result of more or less random combinations of terms such as "communications", "management", "engineer", "system", "planning", "director", "creative", "development", "designer", "project", "strategy", "consultant", "product", "investigation", "coordinator", etc. The idea is that the symbolic analyst, more than a professional career, has temporal jobs/occupations and is part of groups or task-teams that are continuously created and dissolved, according to the rhythm of tasks at hand. The very idea of "making a career" loses meaning in this context. The symbolic analyst is a part, rather, of what Gibbons and Gibbons et al has been calling "Mode II of production and utilization of knowledge", characterized by the following features:

— Knowledge is produced in the "application contexts" in which it is being employed, hence in a sense of utilitarianism and sensitiveness to demands;

— It is habitually "trans-disciplinary" in character, and is driven more by the problem than by the discipline, being an object of transference to new problems instead of being channeled via publications, thus accompanying is practitioners, who perform within highly dynamic networks;

— It is produced and used within a "frame of institutional diversity", which means that there are more sites, very different from each other and the purely academic, in which this knowledge is generated, together with an intense use of electronic communication networks;

— Within these conditions, knowledge assumes, moreover, greater accountability, in the sense that the activities of knowledge act upon high-profile problems (health, the environment, poverty, procreation, etc.), positing permanent attention to the demands and interests of groups linked to these problems - for example, in the definition of problems and the dissemination of solutions; and finally,

— There is also a "more diversified quality-control": to peer assessment are added criteria of the market, of social acceptability, of ethics, etc.

— Education finds itself in tension vis-à-vis work, which is going through profound changes, both from the side of the distribution of occupations between economic sectors, the transformation of job content, skill, knowledge, and ability requirements, and, particularly, the performance of symbolic analysts, whose labor market tends to be globally structured, affecting in particular the link between universities and other institutions of higher education and their economic and social surroundings.

The technological context within which education has unfolded has been highly stable throughout time- more so than the contexts of information and knowledge. After the invention of printing, schools adjusted technologically to broadcasting of lectures, texts, pencils, and to chalk and blackboard. Only late in time did they add the overhead projector and, later, the TV and VCR.

But all of this has begun to change rapidly and deeply with the global spread of NICT. One of the major constants of school life - the isolation of schools - has begun to diminish through the connection of schools to networks; just as one of the constituent principals of learning (plane, or linear text) begins to be replaced by hypertext. In short, we are in transit between low-tech and high-tech education. This is expressed in the famous continuum of learning technologies of Tapscott, where they are ordered from left to right according to the degree of control that students have over learning.

The learning technologies represented go from the analog to the digital, from broadcasts to interactive forms, and from exogenous control of processes (away from the student) to autonomous control (by the student).

TV represents the medium "in which all intelligence finds its point of origin" of transmission; in this case, the teacher. Video tapes represent a step forward, but permit greater control on the part of the user (when and where to reproduce them). Books may be taken from one place to the other, and texts read in the order that one desires.

Face-to-face classes can have a larger interactive component. But the leap occurred, according to Tapscott, recently with the advent of "digital media", starting with the most rudimentary types of computer-aided instruction: routines, pre-programmed tutorials, and teaching games, all of which permit a greater degree of self-control of the process on the part of the student, and various interactive forms. The latter have increased with the use of hyper-media -which employ a combination of media - being able to result in on-line forums, MUDs (multi-user domain), which are sites on the Net where users create and participate, in real time, in a virtual situation. "Soon your kids studying science will be able to meet in a troubled bio-region and share data, research, and solutions, or have a meeting in a space station about the results of an experiment on the impact of gravity on viruses". The next step will be virtual reality simulators for learning and, eventually, the Net as a whole.

Tiffin and Rajasingham predicted this (for now) "last phase" of the continuum, referring to CGVR (computer-generated virtual reality) technologies and their application within a "virtual classroom". Their idea was that "at some time in the first decade of the next millennium - that is to say, during the current decade - it will be possible to generate a virtual version of the kind of classes with which we are familiar".

Such a class may contain electronically configured versions of all of the critical elements for teaching and learning: e-mail for communication between students and between them and their teachers, access to electronic libraries and stores of knowledge, means to enter and to participate in CGVRs in order to develop higher cognitive functions, establishment of small groups or virtual communities for tele-learning, the possibility for each student to progress at his or her own pace and to pass from one level to the other through corresponding examinations when one has acquired the expected skills, etc.

A large number of elements foreseen by Tiffin and Rajasingham when they originally published their book five years ago are now available as currently used technologies. What is not clear, however, is at what speed schools can adopt to new circumstances, making the transition from the analog to the digital world, and thus take advantage of the possibilities offered by NICT is their most advanced versions. Neither is it clear how many schools and families can complete this transit ion nor how many will fall behind, increasing even more the fracture within society. Neither does one currently know with certainty what results and real advantages these technologies will incorporate, nor at what cost for governments and private parties. What already appears evident, at least, is that higher education is changing rapidly through the use of NICT - particularly network technologies.

These not only extend traditional forms of distance education - by correspondence, radio, and television. They also produce a large quantity of programs that employ electronic networks to create, transmit, and deliver advanced information and knowledge. It is estimated that in the United States, more than 3,000 institutions offer on-line courses. Thirty-three states have at least one virtual university.

More than 50% of the courses employ e-mail as a means of communication, and at least one-third use the Net to distribute support materials and resources. Something similar is occurring in other parts of the world. Recently, the Royal Technological University of Melbourne decided to construct, together with private investors, a 50 million dollar campus in Ho Chi Minh City, where they will provide virtual programs with in-person support. For his part, the Prime Minister of France recently announced the creation in Marseilles of a new "great school", as the French call them - on the Internet, that will offer engineering courses specializing in information and communication technologies. This is the French response to the prediction that, by the year 2005, there will be a deficit of 60,000 engineers in this field - considered vital for the country's competitiveness within the European Union and with North America and Japan. Some developing countries are moving in the same direction. In fact, the largest distance learning universities are located in this part of the world - in Turkey, China, Indonesia, India, Thailand, South Africa, and Iran. In addition, the private sector - both academic and business - has successfully entered this area. The Universidad Virtual del Instituto Tecnológico de Monterrey offers 15 masters-level programs using the Internet and tele-conferencing, reaching 50,000 students in Mexico, and has more than 100 support centers located in various Latin American countries. Educor - a South African company - currently employs more than 4,000 instructors who teach using computers and the Internet to reach 300,000 students enrolled in 160 headquarters.

The changes taking place likewise change the competitive scenario within which institutions develop. This is nothing new. Universities have had to continually adapt to their surroundings during almost eight centuries of existence. The difference resides in the magnitude and speed of current change, particularly within the contexts of information, knowledge, and employment. Given the new conditions, it is difficult for universities to maintain their monopolies on information, curricula, or, even, accreditation; which can be, by itself, the central institution of the intellectual system of a nation, as a distinguished sociologist noted more than three decades ago.

However, inst itutions of higher learning are beginning to compete - and upon occasion collaborate - within the new scenario. For example, the famous Open University of England daily bombards young Canadians via e-mail with a message that says, "we offer you academic grades, and actually, we don't care if they are recognized or not in your country; Cambridge and Oxford accept them. And we do it at one-tenth of the cost".

In Brazil, Colombia, Chile, and the Dominican Republic - as well as the Philippines, Indonesia, and South Korea - the private sector accounts for more than 50% of higher education enrollment. Even research is today located in various places and not only in universities, as is shown by the fact that in Canada, the United States, Japan, South Korea, Singapore, Denmark, and Germany, half or more of researchers work in collaboration with the private sector, in contrast with most developing countries where scientists are found mostly in universities. Nevertheless, such described tendencies do not yet cover our system, and this explains, in part, the relative stagnation one observes in Latin American higher education. In contrast to what occurs in more dynamic nations and systems, we continue clinging to the same inward-looking model of analog transmission resistant to differentiation and flexibility, that considers each institution as isolated, rather than part of a network, fearful of competence and with suspicions regarding public-private collaboration.

Diverse World Realities

Finally, in perhaps a less evident manner, education should take into account changes taking place in the immediate cultural context within which it develops; that is, within the context of feelings and meanings that permit it to function in a stable manner in regard to its own participants - students and teachers - and to families and the community. There is a "socialization deficit" within contemporary society that he attributes to a crisis in the function of cultural uniformization of the nation - a classic State and school function - and to the loss in the educability of traditional agents - families, schools, and, we might add, of churches and local communities. There has especially been a decline in the role of the teacher as socializing agent, along with the appearance of new competing modes of socialization, such as television, for example.

This "socialization deficit" does not only have to do with transformations and weaknesses of socialization agents; rather, in a deeper sense, it has to do with "the problem of the weakening of the foundations upon which we define social and personal identities and, on the other, the loss of ideals, the absence of utopias, the lack of meaning". Truly, we live in an era close to the reign of anomie; that is, "a state of extreme uncertainty in which no one knows what behavior to expect of others in each situation".

Modern contractual, atomized societies, without a common base of beliefs, find it difficult to regulate peoples' behavior through norms. Instead of moral integration and an accepted order of sanctions, a normative ambiguity seems to rule. Conservative thought tends to blame these evils on television, as does an author in stating that this medium "has become an instrument for the dissemination of corrupt, demoralizing, and destructive values", having replaced traditional agents for the socialization and transmission of values. It is not true, however, that some media have replaced others. What has happened is that all now exist in a multi-dimensional space, creating the sensation that nothing is fixed and that everything depends on the point of view of the observer. This presents an additional challenge for schools. They will have to assume new roles in a social context the traditional bases of which have deteriorated.

Universities face the reign of anomie under even more complicated conditions, for traditionally they have performed the function of "making sense" of their times. Especially at times of great changes, they have assumed the task of producing a comprehensive synthesis of the new historical situation and of expressing it through an education concept, an institutional design, and a set of practices.

But on the contrary, what one sees currently in Latin America is an extreme incapacity of universities to "think about" and to "express" the changes in society that come with globalization, the scientific and technological revolution, and with the new role that knowledge has begun to play in all areas of society. Contemporary Latin American universities do not in any way represent a synthesis of understanding of our era and its changes. And I do not speak here of a "crisis of the university" in the sense of its organization, governance, management, financing, etc.; it is the very "idea of the university" ' its spirit, so to say - that is out of line, unbalanced, in regard to its surroundings.

Stated in an exaggerated and polemic fashion (given that these are reflections, glints of intuition, speculations, and conjectures): our universities are of the worlds of the 19 th and the beginning of the 20 th centuries, and they are probably dying before our eyes. Why? Because they no longer correspond to any creative/productive/real/ relevant/ relation in the equation between external challenges (changes in surroundings) and ability to respond. From this point of view, they are changing into phantasmagoric figures: they can undoubtedly still educate, and do some interesting, even valuable things. But they are unable to express reflectively and institutionally the worlds of possibilities that are appearing around them and to embody these worlds in a new conception of themselves and in new working practices and modalities.

We should remember here what was said about German universities between the wars: that they were unable to provide a forum that was needed to bring together in a coherent manner, those elements necessary for a true understanding of the position of the German nation. In the words of a knowledgeable student of

Germany and of its intellectual life, "this was a failure of those who [...] were professionally charged with maintaining the coherence of the intellectual life of the Nation; a failure of the universities.

Today, we undoubtedly face a great challenge: how to conceptualize and create - within a society that is profoundly and rapidly changing - a model of a post-national, post-State, university; a university organized around networks, that takes advantage of the full potential of NICT, rests upon sold disciplinary bases, but at the same time being "trans" in many respects, that together with academic research embraces the so-called Mode II of knowledge production, that trains symbolic analysts able to effectively enter the world arena, that is able to compete with the university conglomerates to the North, and, at the same time, maintains a local and regional presence and roots. In short, we should say in closing this chapter that it appears perfectly possible to speak of the impact of globalization on education in a better-fitting context than that of "grand effects". We refer to the area of immediate and proximate contexts within which education develops. In a rapid fashion, we have indicated that education systems in Latin America face a profound and accelerated change of these contexts, at least in the dimensions of access to information, management of knowledge, the relation with the labor market, employment of technologies, and socialization in the culture of the times. Such changes will oblige systems to change in order to adapt to the new scenario.

The future of education in Latin America will be shaped by the form that these changes take, by more or less success in carrying them forward, and by the accumulated consequences of the failures.

Education in the New Context

In this section we will briefly treat - almost as notes, sketches, discussion points - some of the principal paths that education systems follow in order to adapt to the changes in context that we have described above - or rather, the ways that some thinkers imagine that these adaptations will occur. We may say that there are three basic strategies that countries are following -together- to adapt education to the changes in context in which it is involved:

— Toward life-long learning for all (LLLA)

— Toward distance education and distributed learning

— Toward the inst itutionalization of networks

Life;ong Learning for All

"The new idea underpinning 'lifelong learning for all' goes beyond providing a second or third chance for adults and proposes that everyone should be able, motivated and actively encouraged to learn throughout life. This view of learning embraces individual and social developments of all kind and in all settings-formally, in schools, vocational, tertiary and adult education institutions, and non-formally, at home, at work, and in the community. The approach is system-wide; it focuses on the standards of knowledge and skills needed by all, regardless of age. As such, it is geared to serve several objectives: to foster personal development, including the use of time outside of work (including in retirement); to strengthen democratic values; to cultivate community life; to maintain social cohesion; and to promote innovation, productivity and economic growth".

Above all, it represents a response to changes in the labor context within which education operates. To a lesser degree, it is also a response to changes in the contexts of technological information and knowledge, and of different realities of life within contemporary society. It is a strategy that is promoted with particular impetus by the OECD.

Distance Education and Distributed Learning

For the medium-term, these represent the major medium for LLLA, which can hardly be imagined without the use of networking technologies. Its development began including all levels of the system - from basic up to post-secondary - but more rapid progress has resulted in the segment of de-regulated higher- level programs. Basically, NICT make possible what Crane calls "lifelong learning-anytime, anywhere, for anyone".

The swift introduction of these technologies has been facilitated by declining costs of technologies, particularly for hardware; its increasing power, as manifested in Moore's Law, and its ever-increasing portability; increasing capacity and speed in links and communications; the use of digital media to simultaneously transmit voice, text, and images; and the development of inter-active communication modalities, which have been facilitated by the development of network technologies. They constitute the basis of a new education revolution and lead us to think that, "overall, rapidly evolving information devices, tools, media, and infrastructures are transforming what we learn, how we acquire this knowledge, and the process by which we evolve our educational institutions".

Above all, they take advantage of the accelerated change in the technological context within which education functions, which, after remaining practically unaltered from the XV until the XX century, has now begun to change rapidly. Thus, distance education and distributed learning are an answer to changes in the contexts of information, knowledge, work, and cultural meaning. It is a strategy promoted, above all, by national governments, particularly in developed countries, and embraced (although at times only tepidly supported) by entities such as UNESCO, The World Bank.

Institutionalisation of Networks

The organization of education follows the configuration rules of society, which in the future, according to Castells will be "a network society". "As a historical trend, dominant functions and processes in the information age are increasingly organized around networks. Networks constitute the new social morphology of our societies, and the diffusion of networking logic substantially modifies the operation and outcomes in processes of production, experience, power, and culture". In fact, LLLA and the full utilization of the potential surrounding NICT will require that education be organized in a very different manner than in the present - which represents the legacy of several centuries of centralism, bureaucratic control, administrative coordination, rigid hierarchy, strong classificatory schemes, putting together of bits and pieces, separation of levels, intense public supervision, exclusive or preferential tax-based financing, etc.

The creation of networks represents a different configuration: with open structures, non-fixed, but changeable limits, multiple connections and communication paths between units and nodes; with a high frequency of contact between them; with non-linear by interwoven hierarchies; with decentralization, flexibility, autonomy of entities and/or base programs; with forms of coordination designed more for the market than for the State, more through accreditation and assessment mechanisms than through means of direct control. This inst itutional modalit y provides mult iple interfaces with that environment as well as greater response capacity and opportunity - the only way to facilitate adaptation to changing contexts of information, knowledge, work, technology, and culture. It represents a strategy that is not promoted as such, although it has a number of supporters in defined areas such as school autonomy (the effective sociology and the school-based management of school decentralization, of flexible contact between levels, programs, and sectors of the education system (a view favored by practically all specialists), etc. If the institutionalization of such education networks - with all of the fluidity imaginable, compared with the rigidity and security that a bureaucratically organized school system provides - can transmit the necessary sense of order and stability when it is threatened by changes. In effect, according to Castells, "the new social order, the network society, increasingly appears to most people as a meta social-disorder. Namely, as an automated, random sequence of events, derived from uncontrollable logic of markets, technology, geopolitical order, or biological determination". Late modernity or post-modernity arrives in the new century as a uncontrolled force.

In such circumstances - proper to risk-based societies and, as we have seen, with a "socialization deficit", a widespread feeling of anomie and a situation in which personal, social, and national identities are threatened - we may ask the question of how schools An open question is if the institutionalization of such education networks - with all of the fluidity imaginable, compared with the rigidity and security that a bureaucratically organized school system provides - can transmit the necessary sense of order and stability when it is threatened by changes. In effect, according to Castells, "the new social order, the network society, increasingly appears to most people as a meta social-disorder. Namely, as an automated, random sequence of events, derived from uncontrollable logic of markets, technology, geopolitical order, or biological determination". Late modernity or post-modernity arrives in the new century as a uncontrolled force.

In such circumstances - proper to risk-based societies and, as we have seen, with a "socialization deficit", a widespread feeling of anomie and a situation in which personal, social, and national identities are threatened- we may ask the question of how schools and education in general) can contribute to the training tasks of varieties of reality; that is, to provide shared cultural meanings that make possible the continuation of community life and social cohesion.

Latin American education faces two enormous challenges. On the one hand, it must complete "pending tasks" of the XX century, such as universal coverage of pre-school, basic, and secondary education; incorporate indigenous populations into the school system; improve the quality of teaching results in basic skills, particularly among the poorest groups of children, young people, and adults; modernize secondary and higher levels of technical education, provide mass access to higher education.

On the other hand, it must make a leap toward the XXI century and carry forward with "new tasks" upon which will depend economic growth, social equity, and cultural integration. It must adapt structures, processes, results, and education policies to deal with changes - due to globalization—that the areas of information, knowledge, work, technology, and cultural meaning will face in the development of the processes of teaching and of learning. Both agendas - of the XX and of the XXI centuries - are exceedingly demanding and costly. To apply them at the same time is a feat that will require considerable effort. Adjusting their goals and paces of implementation will, from here on, be the key to education policy. The risks that will appear under these circumstances are commensurable with the magnitude of the challenges.

— The first of these risks is to remain tied to the agenda of the past century, putting off the agenda of the current century by considering it too futuristic, far from the needs of people, or beyond the reach - above all beyond the means and resources - of a developing country. The danger involved in this option is that of increasing the gap that separates countries with low-tech education from those that have begun to move toward a XXI century agenda. This can only increase the technology and knowledge gap between countries - a gap that represents an enormous threat to the emerging global order. Similarly, such a choice may bring with it a deepening of the fractures within our own societies, separating the high-speed minority that is integrated into globalization from the majority that lives at low-speed and will be excluded from the fruits of globalization.

— In any case, a wall does not separate the two agendas. We may even say that the two share a "common base" - the desire to raise to the maximum in the shortest time possible the abilities of all children and young people so they may master the skills of reading and writing, numeracy. In effect, such abilities are essential for performance within the global information society and their mastery is, as the same time, the most important pending goal of the XX century agenda. For this reason, countries that develop these skills to the maximum in all people in the shortest possible time, will be fulfilling the major promise of the former agenda and will simultaneously create conditions to face the tasks of the future.

— The second risk, that in a sense accompanies the first, is believing that the agenda of the XXI century is defined in terms of ending and providing follow-up for that of the XX century, and that it can only be accomplished once we have fulfilled pending tasks. On the contrary, what developing countries must do is to make use of the NICT - which are key elements, as we have seen of the future agenda - to take this leap forward, thus cutting intermediate stages where possible. It is now possible for a developing country to create from scratch a new school with a new pedagogy that embraces the NICT, without going through the traditional phases of progressive introduction of new technological supports. Similarly, one can imagine a complete education system that, through adequate strategies to foster distance education, distributed learning, and early adoption of the development of networks, can move forward skipping stages, moving toward a higher state of education and life-long learning for all.

— We cannot hope that developing countries will simply imitate those countries that have first adopted high-tech solutions in education, given the fact that the developed countries have done so precisely because they have previously resolved most of the problems the belong to the former phase; that is, those of a XX century agenda. In the case of developing countries, on the contrary, a strategy to solve these problems should include the use of NICT, the inter-connection of schools, and Internet access, as means to make up lost time and to accelerate the development of education.

— An additional risk is to confuse the velocity of developments in technology in the areas of information and communications with the pace - necessarily much slower - at which teaching and learning processes occur. A number of authors have said that it is a grave interpretive error to think of human intelligence as if it were a computer, or to reduce the mind to an intricate process of computational operations. Similarly, it is an error to think of the process of education as merely one of transmission, and subject, therefore, to Moore's Law: increasing powerful and less expensive as the capacity of support technology increases. The education of a person does not, and cannot, take place at this pace; nor can it evolve according to this rule. It cannot be reduced solely to a procedure of "loading" the mind with a certain quantity of information. At their extremes, certain utopian tendencies that accompany the development of NICT seem to imagine that, in the future, it will be possible to connect a mind to some kind of global network that will create some kind of hyper-conscience, or to directly implant a chip in the brain, containing all of the information required to move about in the world like an educated person. Such reductionist and utopian visions disregard the essentially "organic", evolutionary, and, above all, cultural (in the meaning of "making sense") character of education. This character depends, on the one hand, on bio-psychological development, and, on the other, its slow incorporation into the culture of one's group and time. None of this may be artificially accelerated as one can accelerate a particle - nor as one can give velocity to a machine or goad a pack animal.

— A fourth risk that lies on the road to reconciling the two agendas has to do with managing the "architecture" of the education system. The need to make it as flexible as possible - giving it a network structure - may be confused by some with a prescription in favor of doing away with schools - Iván Illich urged during the 1960s. This is not the case, however. Schools are not called upon to disappear in the future. Rather, they should be transformed during their adaptation to new contexts in which they develop teaching and learning processes. Consequently, their position within the system will change in ways that we still cannot imagine, while the balance, quantity, and quality of the relation between school and non-school processes of teaching and learning will change as well.

— An accompanying risk, although in a different direction, of the one we have just mentioned, is the insistence of maintaining unaltered the current architecture of the system under the supposition that any flexibility means fragmentation of the education system, and will lead, eventually, to greater levels of inequality for the population it serves. Such fear is not realistic. Nor has it been proven that increases in flexibility of education systems result necessarily in greater inequality of access, treatment, or results. Furthermore, insisting on maintaining the architecture of the XX century will impede systems from adapting with sufficient speed and commitment to the new tasks of the XXI century. This would be an additional obstacle, given the need that exists to reconcile the two agendas. Today, both require, above all if we wish them to strengthen one another, that education move increasingly into the "third sector". That is, into society - given that neither the market nor the State can "produce it" nor administer it according to the requirements of a society made up as a system of networks.

— In light of the above, we should mention, finally, the risk that the education of the majority will not continue to invest its resources and energies into arresting the negative forces of anomie and the effects of the cultural disintegration of families and communities.

— There are certainly those who fear that in the near future, "the real race in each geographic region of the world will be that between institutions of the third sector and those of the fourth sector for control over local geography, at a time when this will be partially abandoned by government and by companies". This is, without doubt, a risk that globalization and late modernity bring with them, both in developed and in developing nations. Already we see the struggle in the heart of large cities in Latin America for control -

both territorial and cultural - of the local community. Locked in this struggle are, on the one hand, families, schools, neighbors, community groups, churches, sport centers, police, and local authorities, and on the other, gangs, drug traffickers, delinquents, armed bands, and corrupt police. This is an ominous portent of where the current situation can lead if timely steps are not taken. Here, the institution of education has a vital role to play - one that goes beyond the agendas of yesterday and of tomorrow; for comprises one of today's most important tasks.

7

Future of Higher Education in Globalisation

Globalisation can be described as the imitation, adaptation and diffusion of technological innovations as the process of industrialisation spreads from one country to another. That a particular innovation might undermine, or render obsolete, the basis on which a firm stands together with the recognition that this threat might arise from an increasing number of places located anywhere in the world, has the immediate effect of increasing competitive behaviour amongst firms.

Further, competition always launches a discovery process and it follows that an increase in competitive behaviour will manifest itself in the intensification of the search for innovations.

One way of searching is for firms to engage in R&D activities. It is perhaps because R&D is understood to produce new knowledge that it is frequently argued that in the process of innovation, knowledge has become the scarce resource.

So, it might be appropriate to recognise this claim by speaking of innovation as a search for "knowledge solutions" of various kinds. Globalisation, then, describes the spread of industrialisation from one country to another. But, what is spread are innovations that depend increasingly upon more or less specialised knowledge inputs and this, in turn, is driven by competition between firms. What is not often enough recognised is that at any given time competition between firms operates simultaneously at two levels: the level of static competition and the level of dynamic competition.

The presence of static competition drives a firm's to search for efficiency gains by constantly trying to improve the ways in which existing resources are allocated. At this level, the discovery process often involves a degree of R&D activity, sometimes with universities, as firms seek to improve the industrial processes they have adopted and performance characteristics of the products that they currently make. The result is a stream of incremental innovations within the framework a previously chosen set of technologies; what is often described as a design configuration. At the level of static competition, markets operate to choose amongst products and because firms differ in the efficiency with which they operate, there results in each sector, a hierarchy of firms distributed about what is sometimes referred to as "average best practice".

Under dynamic competition, things are very different. Dynamic competition also launches a discovery process but in a different form, in the sense that it is a search for novel design configurations—novel combinations of scientific ideas and technologies—that might form the bases for the long term survival of the firm, should its existing set of technologies—its current design configuration - be attacked by innovations from one quarter or another.

In other words, dynamic competition launches the sort of search behaviour that firms undertake in anticipation of the possibility that from somewhere a knowledge solution will arise which might render their current technological base and associated work force obsolete. But since it is not known what these knowledge solutions will be or where such they may arise from, firms deal with this type of risk by participating in joint activities, often joint research activities. To accomplish this, they join networks, enter alliances and form partnerships of various kinds. In terms of the search process, these collaborations form complex problem-solving sites.

Solutions are pursued collaboratively, involving many participants, and, paradoxically, they often involve competitors. Under dynamic competition, markets operate not to choose between products for there are none yet, but between research groups. And, because groups differ in their creativity, the performance of each research group will depend on its composition. It is, therefore, of the utmost importance for firms which, and how many, research collaborations they join. Globalisation is, in part, about the imitation and adaptation of these "knowledge solutions" as they diffuse from one firm to another and from country to another. For the purposes of this exposition, the main point to note that globalisation because it stimulates dynamic competition drives the proliferation of collaborative problem solving sites as it draws more and more firms into its competitive ambit.

The evidence for this is unequivocal: the numbers of these collaborative ventures are expanding exponentially across a large number of sectors. Of course, the human resources for these collaborative research ventures are drawn the employees of firms, but they also make use of the expertise that lies in a socially distributed knowledge production system which is rapidly acquiring a global dimension. Now, these sites of collaborative research function as "attractors" for the academic community, in part because in many cases they involve research at the leading edge of a disciplinary field, but also because, for many academics, the opportunity to work in these problems solving groups provides an important way for them to utilise and develop their specialist skills.

If one were to describe some of the principal characteristics of research practice in the search for novel design configurations, it could be said that such research is carried out in the context of application, that it is transdisciplinary and that it involves heterogeneous sets of skills. Further, one could note that these ventures utilise flatter organisational structures that are, more often than not, transient. Further, to function effectively these forms of collaborative research also need to elaborate broader forms of quality control.

The spread of globalisation is accompanied by the proliferation of collaborative research arrangements and these ventures are the sites in which new research practices are being developed. Into this process are drawn an increasing number of members of the academic community. In fact, the numbers of academics participating in this type of industry-driven search for involved are already large enough for the experience to begin to "feedback" into, and so affect, the ways in which research is pursued in universities.

Globalisation and the Universities

This tension manifests itself along many dimensions:

- between academics: who seek peer recognition for their participation in what is a recognisably different kind of research activity;
- between academics and the university: for a more differentiated reward structure that recognises different types of research activity;
- between universities: in terms of the prestige of having their faculty deemed sufficiently competent to be admitted to these, often elite, forms of collaborative research; and
- between universities and industry: for sharing of the revenues from intellectual property, which is now more likely to be the outcome, not of individual genius but of the joint production of knowledge by experts of many different kinds.

Globalisation, through the tensions that it introduces into academic life, is touching the nature of the university at its heart: in the research process itself. It should be noted that, so far at least, the drift of academic researchers into collaborative research with industry has not been the outcome of governmental policy or institutional strategy.The decisions of academics to join these types of collaborative research activities has been largely a matter of individual choice. It is what academics seem to want to do; and, it must be said, it is often an attractive option for the best of them. If the universities wish to adjust to these changes in the behaviour of their researches - and it is hard to imagine how they might resist - then they need to modify their recruitment policies, their terms and conditions of work and their reward structures. But the consequence of such modifications have profound implications for universities as institutions. By becoming so deeply involved in the innovation process, universities are being drawn ineluctably closer to industry. But, in doing this, or allowing it to happen, they are in fact also changing the basis of their relationship with the wider society. Can universities enter into this new, closer, relationship with industry and still maintain their status as independent, autonomous institutions dedicated to the public good? They need to take their participation in collaborative research beyond the limited business/ economic context of the search for novel design configurations. They need to develop the procedures, organisational forms and reward structures that will produce a types of science (and scientists) that are sensitive to context, that takes the search for knowledge solutions beyond a dialogue of experts and that embraces wider social participation in the research process. Stated otherwise, and perhaps a bit provocatively, the universities, as institutions, need to make a commitment to move from the production of merely reliable knowledge to, what might be called, the production of socially robust knowledge.

Mastering Globalisation

We all recognize that we live in a world of contradictions. And contradictions can persist for long periods of time. I'm sure you're all aware of George Orwell's famous novel, '1984'. What you may not know is that he invented a new word in that novel: the word doublethink, which provides an interesting characterization of many individuals and organizations

Globalization refers to the process whereby countries become more integrated via movements of goods, capital, labor, and ideas. Trade (the main channel through which globalization is occurring) offers great advantages because it allows each country to specialize in what it does best - in other words, to have a more refined international division of labor. Globalization has both facilitated, and been facilitated by, advances in information and communications technology. These advances, coupled with the increasingly refined international division of labor, have meant that new ideas are quickly brought to fruition and new technologies developed, and superseded, more rapidly than at any other time in history. Knowledge has become an increasingly important determinant of the wealth of nations, and access to knowledge, and the ability to disseminate it, has become a major source of competitive advantage. Higher education can be a vital tool for helping developing countries to benefit from globalization. So far, most technological advances have been borne in the developed world.

Although rich countries are home to just 15% of the world's population, they are responsible for over 90% of patents granted. If developing countries aspire to catch up, higher education can be a fundamental instrument for speeding that process. Learning how to access ideas and technologies developed elsewhere and put them into practice - skills that higher education is uniquely well-suited to build - can enable developing countries to garner the benefits of globalization without the laborious and costly process of discovery.

Higher education can also help countries attract foreign investment and participate more effectively in international affairs given the technical demands of diplomacy, international commerce and global governance. In other words, higher education can help developing countries use the economic transformation being wrought by globalization to leapfrog stages of development. Globalization, in turn, can help a country benefit from the products of higher education. One of the problems in the Arab world seems to be that, in countries like Egypt and Jordan, many young people are emerging from higher education institutions with no jobs to go to. Rigid labor markets and a failure to connect to global trade routes have led to relative isolation and economic stagnation in much of the Middle East. Having a lot of well-educated young people sitting around with nothing to do can be a recipe for unrest.

Well-managed integration into the global economy, on the other hand, can boost economies, promote foreign investment and create jobs, enabling countries to take advantage of the products of their higher education systems and benefit from their skills and knowledge. Globalization can also help institutions benefit from lessons learned in other countries, and from linking up with foreign institutions to solve problems.

The combination of globalization and higher education offers huge potential for improving living standards. India, for example has taken advantage of globalization by building up its software engineering industry, both in terms of trained software engineers, back office services industry, and new companies and projects. The economies of those parts of India -such as Bangalore and Hyderabad—that have got in on the act are flourishing, and provide a good example of a country using higher education to take advantage of one of the many promising opportunities offered by globalization. Over 80,000 people work in Bangalore's high-tech industry—many of them products of the city's 100 research universities and technical colleges.

IBM, Intel, Microsoft, Oracle and Sun Microsystems have all either set up software development centers or established links with local firms so that they can take advantage of India's supply of well-trained computer graduates. But the international community, and most developing countries themselves, have yet to realize the enormous benefits of higher education.

Large gains have been made in promoting basic and secondary education, but the UN's Millennium Development Goals, and the recent declaration of the World Summit on Sustainable Development in Johannesburg make no mention of tertiary schooling. It is particularly striking that higher education is not mentioned as an instrument for achieving even one of the Millennium Development Goals of the United Nations. A look at the Goals makes it pretty clear that attainment of nearly every one of them will be much easier if a country has a strong and productive higher education system.

The first two goals, for example - halving the proportion of people whose income is less than a dollar a day and the proportion living in hunger by 2015 - are largely reliant on economic development and poverty reduction measures. Without a higher education system, who is going to devise poverty reduction strategies? Who is going to carry out the agricultural research to develop the technologies appropriate for those living off the land? And who is going to put in place policies that promote economic development and negotiate debt relief and access to rich-world markets at the WTO?

The next goal - ensuring universal primary and secondary education - is also reliant on higher education to train the teachers who wi'' ensure that increased quantity of education is matched by improved quality. And this also applies to most of the other goals as well. Empowering women requires, among many other things, women to be able to hold positions of power. Reducing infant mortality requires better-trained medical staff. And reversing the loss of environmental resources needs, among many other knowledge-driven initiatives, research into alternative energy sources. All are also closely linked to educational achievement, and particularly the skills in knowledge development and application that higher education produces.

The point is that higher education offers great opportunities for developing countries to benefit from, and help direct the process of globalization. It can contribute to achieving the Millennium Development Goals, and it can empower countries to adopt new technology to meet domestic needs and help them catch up with the global economy. Unfortunately, this need for higher education in developing countries is going largely unmet. In much of the developing world, higher education delivery is woefully unsuited to the demands of globalization. Existing systems satisfy neither the requirements of the global labor market nor domestic social and economic needs. Here are just three of the main issues:

— Where today's world requires problem-solving skills and flexibility, many of today's developing country universities focus on rote learning, where memory, and not creativity and curiosity, is rewarded. In a fast-changing world, higher education institutions must teach their students not only what is known now, but also how to keep their knowledge up to date. Flexibility and a grasp of new knowledge-gathering technologies are vital, but sadly lacking in most of the developing world.

— Equally important is the failure of curricula to encompass the knowledge, skills, and perspectives students need to know. As the recent Task Force on Higher Education and Society put it, infrastructure constraints and a reliance on tradition have left many arts and humanities graduates ensconced in the ranks of "educated unemployment".

— Higher education systems are failing to grab hold of the opportunities offered by global integration.

Globalization is allowing people to burrow out of the confines of their own institutions and link up with others to solve problems, but cross-institutional and cross-border networks, which offer great promise for promoting scientific innovation appropriate to developing countries' needs, are as yet few and far between.

The Task Force on Higher Education and Society, which was co-convened by UNESCO and the World Bank in 1997, suggested that, "urgent action to expand the quantity and improve the quality of higher education in developing countries should be a top development priority." Higher education, the states, "is to a knowledge economy as primary education is to an agrarian economy and secondary education is to an industrial economy." The Task Force was something of a landmark in higher education thinking. World Bank President James Wolfensohn described it as a "wonderful road map" for development policy makers. "Well educated people from the developing world," he said in launching "can be a powerful force for change, but they need schools and academic opportunities in their own countries".

Higher education and the public interest

The first main theme covered higher education and the public interest. Modern ignorance about higher education has been led by economists - the tribe of dismal scientists. Our habit of knowing the price of everything, but the value of nothing, has led us into an incredibly simplistic way of assessing the return on investments in higher education. There is not sufficient time to explain the calculation in full - but the basic flaw is to measure the return on education exclusively through wage differentials.

Take someone who has no education, someone who has been to primary school, someone who has completed secondary school, and someone with a university degree. How much more does each earn than the previous? These differentials are then compared to the incremental amounts invested in their education to find the return. The results generally suggest that higher education yields a lower return than primary or secondary education - and they have been used to justify the skewing of government budgets (and developments funds) away from higher education institutions.

The rate of return calculations are flawed because they do not take account of the full range of benefits to those who receive higher education. For example, higher education can enhance health and reduce fertility - so the private benefits to the individual are not just the direct labor productivity benefits, as the rate of return analysis suggests. The Task Force took a much broader view of the benefits of higher education than mere rate of return. Higher education obviously confers benefits above and beyond enhancing the incomes of those who receive their degrees. And many of these benefits take the form of public goods, such as the contribution of higher education to enterprise, leadership, governance, culture, and participatory democracy, and its potential for lifting the disadvantaged out of poverty. These are all vital building blocks for stronger economies and societies and all routes by which the benefit of investment in higher education multiplies throughout society.

Systems of higher education

The second main theme of the Task Force relates to the need to adopt a system-wide perspective on higher education. Thinking about systems forces countries to focus on the forest as well as the trees - to view the structure and operation of higher education institutions in concert, not just individually. Our view of higher education systems encompasses everything from public research universities to private vocational schools. It addresses the place of these institutions vis-à-vis each other, as well as their links to the rest of the education system and the broader society. Such a perspective lends itself naturally to the development of a rational and stratified system of higher education in the public interest, with different types of institution, from research universities to vocational colleges, dedicated to different missions. Links to higher education institutions in other countries are also becoming increasingly important.

Governance

Governance was the third key theme - by which we mean the arrangements, both formal and informal, that allow the higher education "team" to function. Many of the people who gave evidence to the Task Force pinpointed this as the key problem impeding the effectiveness of higher education institutions. And so we developed a set of principles of good governance, such as academic freedom, autonomy, the need for monitoring and accountability, meritocratic selection, and so on. And we also describe a set of tools for converting these ivory tower principles to action, ranging from specific mechanisms for hiring and promoting faculty and appointing university administrators, to boards of trustees, faculty councils, institutional handbooks, and visiting committees.

Science and technology

Science presents a unique set of challenges for universities across the world. First, basic science is, itself, a public good. Basic scientific inquiry often needs huge investment to deliver long term, but highly uncertain, benefits. The market is not very good at funding this research on its own - especially when the benefits will be felt by the poor more than the rich. As has often been noted, in today's world it can be easier to find funding for research into a new dandruff shampoo than it is to try and develop a cure for malaria.

The way that scientific knowledge is produced is changing rapidly. Increasingly science is done across organizational and disciplinary boundaries, it involves public and private sector participation, and it is often directed towards working in teams to solve a strategically important problem, such as developing an HIV/AIDS vaccine, rather than having individual scientists working alone in a relatively uncoordinated manner in their laboratories.

Scientific progress is leading to growing uncertainty, rather than certainty. The furor over genetically-modified foods - which ties together cutting edge science, big business, and globalization into a heady cocktail - is a perfect example of how difficult it has become to understand where a particular scientific advance is taking us. The relationship between science and society is becoming increasingly vexed - because increasingly experts must admit that they "really don't know." These three factors mean that universities must be substantially more flexible and fleet of foot if they are to fund science adequately, pull together the highest caliber of scientific teams, build curricula relevant to modern societies, and maintain public support for their scientific research. These problems are compounded in many developing countries, where, due to weak human resources, inadequate equipment, a lack of connectivity to the rest of the research world and many other factors, the science and technology base is currently low.

The Task Force believes that developing such a base is no longer optional, but is becoming mandatory for all countries trying to compete in the global knowledge economy.

The importance of general education

The final theme is the importance of a general education. General education emphasizes the development of the whole individual, and not just their occupational training. It highlights the ability to think, communicate, and learn; and to adopt a broad historical, comparative, and disciplinary perspective on different issues. And it is a foundation for later, more specialized, study. The Task

Force urges the introduction - or in a few cases the expansion - of high-quality general education in developing countries.

Such an education is not for all students, but it is in each country's public interest to have individuals who can operate at a high intellectual level in rapidly changing times - whether that involves negotiating with the International Monetary Fund, deciding whether to import generic AIDS drugs, deliberating on the ethical issues surrounding genetically modified food, or acting to develop a national legal system that can robustly protect fundamental human rights.

The content of general education curricula will naturally vary across countries. For example, South Africa should not blindly adopt the conception that exists, for example, here in Canada. Rather, it should take lessons learned elsewhere and adapt them to the needs of South African society. South Africa, where English is widely spoken, for example, may not need the same language courses as a country like Korea. It may, however, need more courses in building strong institutions, so someone educated in subjects like law, philosophy, economics and politics might be relatively more important. Designing a general education program offers the opportunity to ask fundamental questions about what matters to a particular society. It offers the opportunity to focus on a country's history, its culture, and its values. Doing this will help energize the whole higher education system - and, in time, change the way a society thinks about itself too.

The Task Force wasn't the first time a general education has been trumpeted. The key suggestions was that the top 4 or 5 of the 50 public universities establish what we called "honors programs" that would provide a high quality general education to a relatively small number of students per year. The goal would be for those students to obtain a training that would enable them to move easily into top international graduate programs, and eventually return to lead the country's development process. But this suggestion, which we had worked out in great detail, failed to take account of Indonesia's strong egalitarian values.

In other words, giving special training to the most promising students was seen as politically unacceptable. We also suspect that the resistance we encountered was compounded by some of Indonesia's prospective leaders (people in the 30-45 age range) feeling threatened by an ostensibly better trained younger generation. So what seemed a perfectly good and natural suggestion came to nothing because it failed to anticipate and address the realities of Indonesian politics and power.

Implementation

This example is a good segue to the third and final point I'd like to address -implementation. Good ideas by themselves are simply not enough. The field of international development is littered with sensible policy suggestions that have come to nothing in practice. There's a contradiction here - both in the development arena as a whole and higher education in particular - where much more time is spent discussing policy design than how the policy is actually going to be implemented. Some of the difficulties implementing new higher education policies in the era of globalization, would like to briefly consider two issues: curriculum reform and brain drain.

Curriculum reform is widely recognized as being necessary if higher education institutions in developing countries are to produce graduates capable of participating and competing in our emerging global society. But curriculum reform is usually seen as purely a technical problem, as distinct from a political one. In fact it is both a technical and a political problem and the failure to recognize the political aspects of curriculum reform is usually the cause of its undoing. In many cases, the failure of curriculum reform can be ascribed to the adoption of a top-down committee approach. Stakeholder involvement is vital to curriculum design and reform, and leaving out interested and affected parties can be fatal.

All parties with an interest in reform (including teachers, students, administrators, employers and donors) must be encouraged to voice their views - and current faculty in particular must be handled with care, as they are often the ones who feel most threatened by curriculum change. Without this widespread involvement, reformers will fail to bring on board the very people responsible for curriculum delivery. The political obstacles to reform are also highlighted by the brain drain issue. Highly trained human resources can be bought, and they can be bought more easily now because there is more mobility. Students who are skilled in the development and acquisition of knowledge are tempting targets for firms wishing either to get an edge over their competition and for governments and international development organizations needing to fill vacant posts.

For developing countries, this has led to concerns over brain drain, where students whose education has been paid for by a developing-world government take the skills they have acquired abroad, and thereafter contribute little but remittances to their home country. Brain drain makes arguing the case for investment in higher education difficult.

If a sizable number of a country's best students, whose education has been funded out of the public purse, emigrate as soon as they leave college, what benefit has the country reaped from the investment? Questions like this pose serious threats to the reform process. Unless brain drain is considered at the policy development stage, it may come to complicate decisions about investment in higher education and it could provoke strong political opposition.

To reiterate, the point here is that consideration of the politics of reform as well as its technical aspects is crucial. As in much of the rest of the developing world, Pakistan had traditionally taken education to mean predominantly primary and secondary schooling. Both quantity and quality of higher education delivery were woefully inadequate for the country's needs. Governance and management structures and practices, inefficient use of resources, inadequate funding, poor recruitment practices, a lack of attention to research, and the politicization of faculty, staff and students all blocked the path to efficient delivery. So reform was urgently needed. The complex political situation in Pakistan also complicates reform. The country is effectively ruled by a military dictatorship and a fairly chaotic bureaucracy which makes it difficult to achieve anything quickly - not a promising context for implementing a far-reaching reform process. Recently, a group of reform-minded Pakistanis got together. They included representatives from academia, civil society, business, and the Boston Group - an American-based Pakistani think tank.

And not only did they address the usual technical aspects of reform, they were also savvy enough to confront the political aspects of reform and its implementation. To be sure, they made recommendations on technical matters such as the length of Bachelor's degrees, how much new funding was required (and the creation of an endowment to help raise it), delinking faculty pay from the Government's pay scales, and peer review of faculty to ensure that excellence is rewarded. But they also dealt thoughtfully, systematically, and respectfully with the opponents of change, which consisted of a formidable array of higher education institutions reluctant to adapt, politicians and government officials opposed to the involvement of the Boston Group, and many people opposed to President Musharraf's regime in general.

In order to effect change in such a system, the Pakistan Higher Education Task Force relied on what they describe as an entrepreneurial model. This model seeks to promote and encourage "social entrepreneurs", who seek out "strategic points of entry" into the reform process. So instead of trying to get everybody lined up together at the outset and then undertake every part of the reform process at once, individuals and small groups take the initiative and, by effecting change in one small part of the system, attempt to trigger larger changes in other areas. In this model, it is possible to initiate reform without government support, and even without the support of the whole higher education community. By creating and promoting early success stories, you encourage others to take up the gauntlet and build the momentum that will eventually get the politicians' attention.

Co-Chair of the Task Force, neatly summed up this model by quoting Napoleon's battle strategy: "On s'engage, et puis on voit." The Pakistan Task Force model appears to have made a favorable impression on the country's leaders. On hearing and recommendations of the Task Force, President Musharraf announced an immediate 1 billion rupee increase - an increase of one third over the previous budget - in the budget allocation for public universities in the current fiscal year. He also approved the establishment of a Higher Education Commission and an overall doubling of government grants to higher education by 2004-05.

Bibliography

Barnett, R., *The Coming of the Global Village: a tale of two enquiries,* Oxford Review of Education, 25, 3, 293-306, 1999.

Crafts, Nicholas, Globalisation and Growth in the Twentieth-Century, IMF Working Paper, WP/00/44, Washington DC, April 2000.

Dessus, Sebastien, Fukasaku, Kiichiro, and Safadi, Raed., "Policy Brief No. 18: Multilateral Tariff Liberalisation and the Developing Countries", OECD Development Centre. OECD, 1999.

DFID, "Globalisation and Sustainable Development: Issues Paper for DFID", DFID Globalisation Issues Paper, 2000.

DFID, "Globalisation, Water Resources and the Poor", Rural Livelihoods Department Paper, 2000.

DFID, "The Relationship of trade and competition policy to development and economic growth", Background Paper for Competition Policy Round Table 2000.

FitzGerald, Valpy, *Globalisation and poor countries: The role of private capital flows.* QEH, University of Oxford, 2000.

Greenhalgh, Peter, and Kleih, Ulrich, *Globalisation and the Liberalisation of Agricultural Trade; the Impact on Small Farmers in Developing Countries.* University of Greenwich, 2000.

Hirst, P. and Thompson, G., *Globalisation in Question: The International Economy and the Possibilities of Governance,* 2nd edn., Cambridge: Polity Press, 1999.

Jenkins, Rhys, and Barton, Jonathan, "Globalisation and Environment: Opportunities and Threats", Paper Commissioned by DFID (CNTR: 2000 0399) UK: Globalisation Papers. University of East Anglia, 2000.

Micklewait, John, and Woolridge, Adrian, "Restating the Case for Globalisation", 2000.

Mittelman, J. H. (ed.), *Globalisation: Critical Reflections*, Boulder, Colo.: Lynne Rienner, 1996.

Newell, Peter, "Globalisation and the Environment: Issues and Opportunities", DFID, Rural Livelihoods Department Paper. DFID/IDS, 2000.

Ohmae, K., *The Borderless World: Power and Strategy in the Interlinked Economy*, London: Fontana, 1990.

Page, Sheila, Bussolo, Maurizio, Richards, Michael, and Lecompte, Henri Bernard Solignac. 2000. "Globalisation, Environment Change and Poverty", Report prepared for DFID (CNTR 2000 0400). ODI.

Robertson, R., *Globalisation: Social Theory and Global Culture*, London: Sage, 1992.

Rodrik, Dani., "The New global Economy and Developing Countries: Making Openness Work" Summary Paper by Dani Rodrik, 1999.

Skutsch, John, "Globalisation and Liberalisation of Agricultural Trade and Investment Impact on Small Farmers in Developing Countries", DFID, Rural Livelihoods Department Paper. DFID/HR Wallingford, 2000.

Taylor, J C, Flexible Delivery: The Globalisation of Lifelong Learning, *Indian Journal of Open Learning*, 7 (1), 55, 1998.

Williams, Jim, *A few thoughts on Globalisation and the Environment*. NRI, 2000.